Property and Finance on the Post-Brexit London

C000072515

A guide to the contemporary London stage as well as an argument about its future, the book walks readers through the city's performance spaces following the Brexit vote.

Austerity-era London theatre is suffused with the belief that private ownership defines full citizenship, its perspective narrowing to what an affluent audience might find relatable. From pub theatres to the National, Michael Meeuwis reveals how what gets put on in London interacts with the daily life of the neighbourhoods in which they are set.

This study addresses global theatregoers, as well as students and scholars across theatre and performance studies—particularly those interested in UK culture after Brexit, urban geography, class, and theatrical economics.

Michael Meeuwis is Associate Professor in the Department of English and Comparative Literary Studies at the University of Warwick, Coventry, UK. He is a literary historian of the British eighteenth through twenty-first centuries, with an ongoing interest in theatre and performance; or, a theatre historian with a side hustle in literature.

Property and Finance on the Post-Brexit London Stage

We Want What You Have

Michael Meeuwis

LONDON AND NEW YORK

First published 2021
by Routledge
2 Park Square, Milton Park, Abingdon, Oxon OX14 4RN

and by Routledge
52 Vanderbilt Avenue, New York, NY 10017

Routledge is an imprint of the Taylor & Francis Group, an informa business

British Library Cataloguing-in-Publication Data
A catalogue record for this book is available from the British Library

Library of Congress Cataloging-in-Publication Data
A catalog record for this book has been requested

ISBN: 978-0-367-54802-5 (hbk)
ISBN: 978-1-003-09065-6 (ebk)

Typeset in Times New Roman
by Apex CoVantage, LLC

Contents

Acknowledgement

First and foremost, thanks to my Warwick department and its residents. This book would be unimaginable without the support and real estate giftage of Tina Lupton, in London and Copenhagen—still, truly, sorry about the door. And Stephen Shapiro one day said, "I realized I wanted to write about all the television I was watching"—whence, the idea for this book. Myka Tucker-Abramson was there for the Malteasers, and a great deal of spoon-feeding about economics. Liz Barrie finally convinced me that this was a viable project, not that any of what follows is her fault. For conversation ideas about the book project specifically I'd like to thank Ross Forman, Matt Franks, Nadine Holdsworth, Tony Howard, Graeme Macdonald, Pablo Mukherjee, Steve Purcell, Jonathan Schroeder, Rochelle Sibley, Mark Storey, Rashmi Varma, and Chantal Wright. Emma Mason has dealt with a string of disasters as both my mentor and Head of Department; Kirsty Hooper, simply as a mentor. I'd like to thank all of my colleagues for indulging this at a 2018 Warwick Research symposium; all of my students in EN107, way back in 2015, for listening to my thoughts on *Roots* while I sorted out which one my elbow was, and, recently, to Conor Seery and Victoria Sparkes in EN926: The British Dramatist.

In London, Julia Ng read more of this project than anyone else—thanks, in particular, for the aesthetic theory stuff. Thanks also to the staff at the Audience Club (shhh), to Jen Harvie, Issy Harvey, Tim Loveridge, Dan Rebellato, ShzrEe Tan, Narmada Thiranagama, and Diana Zhang. Internationally, this project benefited from ideas from Sarah Balkin, Andrew Broughton, Emine Fisek, Michael Gamer, Sebastian Lecourt, Stephen Ross, Kim Solga, and Tom Perrin.

Thanks to Laura Hussey, my editor at Routledge, and to three anonymous reviewers.

Introduction

Rooting for the house

Rooting for the Yankees is like going into a casino and rooting for the house.
—Doug Stanhope

1 Interrupted motion

In John Lanchester's novel *Capital* (2012), the residents of a street in recently gentrified south London receive threatening postcards through their mailboxes: "We want what you have."[1] London is a widely envied city: a lot of people want to live here. They may desire a fantasy London, but this fantasy has had extremely real implications for those who live here, maybe most acutely in terms of the cost of living. Those who own property become pleased with themselves for doing so; those who don't, aspire frantically to make the dream a reality. Lanchester himself has been far from retiring about tracking the value of his own South London house in print.[2] Chris Hamnett, writing in 2003, puts the matter starkly: "In the space of forty years Inner London has been transformed from a city dominated by private renting, to one where council renting became the single largest tenure in 1981, to one where home ownership is the largest tenure" (126).[3] In this, London reflects the broadest tendencies in our current world moment's dominant neoliberalism, with its emphasis on "private property owners" and an ownership model applied to public services in general.[4] *We Want What You Have* tracks the normalisation of middle-class home ownership in London theatre of the late 2010s: how what Anita Biressi and Heather Nunn term the "lifeblood" of 1980s Conservatism became a default worldview even in progressive theatre venues.[5] While Brexit raged around us, theatregoing Londoners focused our communal anxieties on property. What was lost, frequently, was an imagination of how things could be, otherwise and elsewhere.

There was a moment in Arnold Wesker's *Roots* (1958) that I used to make fun of with students in America—before, I must admit, I really knew what I was talking about. One of the seminal kitchen-sink dramas, *Roots* shows a working-class woman, Beatie Bryant, returning to her home in Norfolk to confront her closed-minded family. Notable in its time for its use of regional dialect and setting, Wesker's play ends with Beatie, humiliated, nevertheless coming to a profound personal realisation. "D'you hear that?," she says to her indifferent family: "D'you hear it? Did you listen to me? I'm talking." For the first time, as she understands herself, she's not repeating back what she's heard from others: from her mustn't-grumble, conformist family; from her unreliable socialist boyfriend Ronnie. Without specifying exactly what she means, she concludes the play, in what is basically an aside to the audience: "[I]t's happening to me, I can feel it's happened, I'm beginning, on my own two feet—I'm beginning."[6] As the stage directions tell us, *Whatever she will do they will continue to live as before as BEATIE stands alone—articulate at last.*[7] We do not know if Beatie's self-realisation will do anything practical in her world. It certainly seems unlikely to win over her family. And yet, disadvantaged by gender, class, and region, Beatie has learned to "articulate" herself. She did so at a major London venue, where a wide range of audiences could potentially see her; the script in which she did so remains on the syllabus.

When it transferred to London's Royal Court in 1958, then, *Roots* made a claim about the future whose institutional support—performance at a subsidised venue, and enshrinement on syllabi—meant that it has endured. Dan Rebellato notes a "frustrating vagueness" behind what *Roots* and plays like it were actually proposing—and, indeed, it's hard to say what exactly Wesker intends.[8] Nevertheless, seen from 60 years on, when so many publicly assisted futures seem unavailable, I believe we can also perceive this vagueness as a feature. *Roots'* claim in its very inchoateness was larger than simply saying that women, or those economically disadvantaged, or those from particular regions, needed their representative time on the stage. By leaving what Beatie wants imprecise—by implying she still needs to figure this out—Wesker leaves open a moment that was *queer*, in the expansive sense proposed by Eve Sedgwick: "a continuing moment, movement, motive—recurrent, eddying, troublant," that leaves irresolute an "open mesh of possibilities, gaps, overlaps, dissonances and resonances."[9] Writing in 1958, Wesker was leaving open what might yet happen for those from a range of underrepresented backgrounds in the welfare state to come. Beatie did not know what she wanted to be yet; she just knew that she wanted it.

This book argues that the imagination of future possibilities and collective sympathies on the late-2010s London stage were too often foreclosed by an insistence on the hard facts of property ownership. In my afterword, I describe this as a dominant narrative present in theatre of the last ten years—and a real shift in the history of the English stage. This book, however, focuses primarily on performances in the years following the 2016 Brexit decision. As Katie Beswick notes, London's housing culture "has resulted in a situation where those without the economic means to buy their own property are displaced and disenfranchised."[10] Much theatre, dismayingly, extended this displacement into the representational realm. Anxiety was classed upwards: the bourgeois became the new precariat, and the lower classes simply disappeared.[11] Even when directly criticising the "bourgeois virtues" of contemporary neoliberalism, performances in London addressed it as inevitable.[12] Philip Ridley's *Radiant Vermin* (2015), which transferred to the Soho Theatre following its first performance at the Tobacco Factory Theatre, Bristol, shows a young married couple murdering a homeless person in order to obtain their "*dream* home"—but ends with their case worker, having sent them on their way to another property, addressing the audience as the next murderers-for-housing: "You're here because *I* summoned you. Why? Because I have a bagful of new contracts."[13] As Beswick notes, many other London theatres structurally presume a middle-class audience.[14] To be present in an established London theatre in the later part of this decade was, often, to be presumed in this way. A 2016 report on England's theatres commissioned by the Arts Council notes a "range of psychosocial barriers to attendance, linked to factors such as early socialisation, issues of class and ethnicity."[15] The fact that mainstream theatres keep telling certain sorts of stories can and does exclude large groups of people.

"London stage," a term I use throughout, is not without problems. I address for the most part productions in the more central parts of London, TFL zones one and two, at venues specifically designated as theatres. This project would look very different if it were, say, a longitudinal study of Brexit-era new work at the Battersea Art Centre, a South London arts space, whose mandate is to produce new work from community and underrepresented groups; or the work of a company like SPID Theatre, located in a council high-rise in Ladbroke Grove and primarily focused on "high quality community theatre in housing estates."[16] What I mean by "London stage" is closer to Beswick's definition of "mainstream" theatre: "a scripted piece of theatre, primarily performed in subsidized building-based theatre venues."[17]

We Want What You Have addresses individual performances of scripted plays in terms of local conditions: the recent histories of certain neighbourhoods, and my own experiences in them. Because scripts can travel more readily than performances, and these mainstream theatres have better and more sustained links to publishing houses, scripted theatre originating in these places has a long reach. I came to the term *autoethnography*, the incorporation of theorised personal experience in analytical academic writing, late in this project.[18] But it conveys my personal stakes, as someone who moved to London during the period that the book surveys after a long time studying the city's drama overseas. I am myself one of neoliberalism's favoured citizens, one of those "skilled international migrants from developed countries."[19] (Even if "theatre historian" is not the classical subject-position of hypercapitalism.) Being, rather hilariously, from London, Ontario, some of my earliest connections to daily experience in *this* London involved reading such narrative dramas. I wanted this kind of "proper" theatre, something that seemed historical and cultured to a desperately provincial sensibility, before I knew there were even alternatives. Some of the unpacking of London neighbourhoods, cultural references, and dominant narrative tendencies that my project undertakes unfolds with an audience like myself in mind. Nevertheless, I am also interested in these venues because they are those with the widest audiences, both within London and from around the world. Mainstream theatres substantiate London's role as what Nigel Thrift calls a "centre of interpretation": a place where cultural agendas are considered and set.[20]

In what follows, I examine a range of theatrical performances across London during the Brexit interregnum: the time between the country's decision to leave the European Union on 23 June 2016 and the country's eventual departure on 31 January 2020. During this time period, performances across a variety of mainstream venues emphasised property ownership in everything from plot to staging choices. London's theatre, once potentially a space for a wider debate and reflection, has been nudged by recent arts policy into reconstituting rather than criticising the class outlook of those people already most likely to go to the theatre.[21]

The resounding Conservative victory in the December 2019 national elections reinforced anew the distance between London's politics and that of much of the rest of the country, with the traditional left-wing Labour Party mostly successful only in the metropolis and other larger urban centres. England over these last five years has evinced a problem talking to itself, amidst what Fintan O'Toole calls "the unravelling of an imagined community": the end of the country's ability to imagine shared assumptions, beliefs, aspirations, and stories. The causes for this are legion: "profound regional inequalities within England itself; the generational divergence of values and aspirations; the undermining of the welfare state and its promise of shared citizenship; the contempt for the poor and vulnerable expressed through austerity."[22] As I will demonstrate, property ownership can be found near the heart of all of these issues. Nevertheless, the party espousing further privatisation— an entrenchment of among other things private property ownership—won the last election commandingly, in particular by appealing to working-class voters in areas long held by Labour. Plenty in London, too, voted Conservative, even though the city returned mostly Labour MPs.

I appreciate the extent to which these plays, then, reflect an overwhelming fact about our times—but theatre can do more than just reflect. Property ownership, like the post-Thatcherite political paradigm more generally, has broken down traditional class and cultural linkages.[23] Those who bought their council housing under the Right to Buy scheme introduced by the Housing Act 1980, recent migrants to the city purchasing a first home, and long-term owning residents of a neighbourhood can all find themselves on the side of ownership. A focus on private property ownership is typical of conservative politics in the twentieth and twenty-first centuries, but an intense interest in property purchase is by no means limited to those of conservative political leanings.[24] My concern in this book is how frequently ownership's new consensus captured the imagination of theatre-makers as well. If a wider consensus between metropole and heartland, south and north, propertied and unpropertied is to be sought, theatre needs to stop scratching the anxieties of its most established, "affluent" audiences.[25]

I'm writing, ultimately, out of a belief that narrative drama in the most traditional sorts of venues can do more to enliven and broaden a national conversation. Mainstream theatre, I believe, has a greater opportunity than other forms to engage audiences with more difficult material than they may be used to encountering.

The issue of private housing has tangled this critical faculty. Anxiety about property presents something that acts like criticism but is in fact class reproduction. Stage techniques that might have been used to shock audiences out of complacency now appear in effect to shock them into it: to convince them that middle-class life is precarious enough that it must be defended at all costs. That "sense of crusading idealism" that Michael Billington notes on the post-war stage is often now replaced in performance by members of the middle classes justifying a fight simply to remain where they are.[26]

2 Interrupted motion: property and the range of sympathy

Let me put this more concretely, in terms of an evening out: 2 October 2017. I had gone to the National Theatre to see an interview with the playwright and director Stephen Berkhoff. Wearing a leather coat and Champion sweatshirt, Berkhoff, at the age of 81 years, was charming and funny and even mildly self-deprecating, switching accents as effortlessly as blinking as he gave accounts of working with English, Irish, and American producers. He was even gracious towards certain work being done in London—although in general British theatre, he announced, "Loves the soporific more than the fantastical."[27] This is the sort of provocation we expect from our elder statesmen—it was why I had come. But Berkhoff supported this contention with something that struck home with me, saying that British theatre took an essentially "narcissistic" attitude towards the country itself. Audiences, he said, went to the theatre to experience "what you see in the mirror": to see their own lives repeated back to them.

For Berkhoff, this style of theatre-making—for which he claimed a grudging respect—denied the fantastical, the unusual, and the unsettling. Geoffrey Colman, the interviewer, suggested that this was the reason why Berkhoff's plays were not receiving the revivals that they should be: that they were premised too much on fantastical interruptions of reality, on imagination and strangeness. Colman lauded, in particular, Berkhoff's 1988 production of Oscar Wilde's *Salome*, which was presented in slow motion. Like Beatie's hung-fire self-articulation at the end of *Roots*, this *Salome* introduced a deliberate interruption into the time of theatrical performance. Interrupted motion, Berkhoff claimed, takes things out of the literal and regular—out of the sort of mere realism in which, he noted, "There will always be a sofa." Familiar furniture emphasises life as it is. Interrupted realism invites imaginative speculation—invites the audience to think about how things might be different, as in a dream or a drug trip.

Yet interrupted motion could also be enlisted into the cause of reflecting the way things are—indeed, into showing their inevitability. Later that night I went to see *Ink* (2017), written by James Graham and directed by Rupert Goold, across the Thames at the Duke of York's Theatre in the West End—a transfer of a play first presented at the Almeida Theatre in Islington. *Ink* concerns the media mogul Rupert Murdoch's purchase and re-formulation of the *Sun*, the downmarket British tabloid that would come to play a huge role in swinging national elections.

I had my cheap tickets, purchased months earlier through a special online deal. This is one way to feel like a savvy Londoner: you mix and mingle with people in similar seats who paid vastly more, looking down your nose at the sort of person who would pay full retail for a ticket or £70 for the bottle of Veuve Cliquot offered in the theatre bar. But we were all stuck in the same perspectival rut: none of us, savvy or not, saw something that proposed that the present-day economy in which we exercised this savvy was anything other than historically inevitable.

Interruptions of motion appeared throughout *Ink*—but used to reinforce, rather than challenge, society's sense of being the way that it is. As Larry Lamb, the *Sun's* new editor, signed up malcontented *Daily Mirror* employees to join his ragtag publication, they joined him in a series of little dances, backed by a company member singing period hits. Susannah Clapp notes that "the action—this is a Rupert Goold trademark—is often on the cusp of a chorus line."[28] I kept thinking of the other part of what Berkhoff had said: about the country seeing only its own face in the theatrical mirror. Here, even the imaginative, speculative possibilities of interrupted motion showed us how things had got to be the way that they are, rather than suggesting how they might become different. Murdoch keeps talking about a "good story," and this is also what the play offered: the sense that the *Sun's* transformation of England was reducible to the actions of a few people, acting for clear-cut reasons.[29] In the last scene, Murdoch tells Lamb that he "learned" a great deal from him: the secrets that he would eventually apply to his Fox Network in America, with its direct influence on the Bush and now Trump presidencies. Lamb even asks Murdoch, in the play's final scene, "Why do I feel like you probably will just somehow outlive us all?"—suggesting that even in the past he could proleptically glimpse Murdoch's long, long influence.[30] It was hard to leave *Ink* and imagine the possibility of change—even the faint possibility that Beatie's story offers.

"It is what it is" is a defining phrase of our political moment, and I had spent my evening watching even anti-realistic techniques subsumed into its grim political realism.[31] And no anxiety defined the performance of this present moment in London theatre more than property ownership. Writing this project started with an odd detail: the casual mention, in a piece set in a 1970s punk squat, that its location was nevertheless privately owned. In what kind of mindset do even anarchists own their own homes? Once I noticed this detail, I started to see it everywhere, even in plays like *Radian Vermin* whose stated purpose was to interrupt audiences' conventional social perceptions. The Almeida, where *Ink* originated, sits near some of the most startling income inequalities in London.[32] The theatre announced that it intended Leo Butler's *Boy* (2016) to show the lives of working-class characters "easily missed amongst the crowd": those left behind in austerity-era London.[33] It did so through startling sustained interruptions not only of motion but of the theatre space, placing the production around a moving walkway onto which complicated sets were assembled and disassembled to show the crowds moving through spaces like the theatre's own mixed-income neighbourhood.

Boy's unnamed main character is white, hoodie-wearing, and mostly silent, living in a London with which he can afford to have few meaningful interactions. Indeed, getting to the Sports Direct in Oxford Street from South London requires a level of ease with and connection to the city that he does not possess. The play demonstrates his anomie—but, around him, property concerns rage. So, in the background of an ensemble scene at a bus shelter, two characters lament, "We've got an income, we're married. / And we're going to be renting for the rest of our lives. Thirteen hundred pounds every month."[34] The background anxiety of where to buy among the aspirational classes—"Isn't there anywhere in Muswell Hill or East Finchley? . . . Finsbury Park? Walthamstow?"—pervades the "crowd" out of which the "overlooked" can emerge (119).

Yet when these "overlooked" speak for any extended length of time, they too reveal themselves as property-obsessed. Across a couple of scenes, the unnamed Boy meets another character designated as "Teenage Boy": a fellow member of the left-behind classes, but better able to articulate his situation.

> "We're going to buy you out, bruv. We're going to buy up all the nice old houses, the schools, the jobs." Bistros and shit, health centres, cycle shops, estate agents. Look around you, G. Moving in, driving up the prices. They're the real migrants, cuz, not them brothers hiding under trucks in Calais. It's these 50k bitches with their recycled bags, driving up and down in their Range Rovers, they're the problem, G. And you know someday there aint going to be no one left? Can't afford to live here no more, so they push us all out to some fucked-up EDL ghetto down in Thornton Heath so that they can go on with their lives without having to look reality in the face and I'm like "What? Fuck off man, the fuck you are. I ain't going nowhere, G." Gotta find your own means, brov. Go work for the other side, you know what I'm saying? Mandem making plenty dollars and they aint going to threaten you with sanctions. Aint going to drive you out of your home or make you work like a bitch until you're sixty fucking five years old. Look at my dad. Working the night shift over in Gatwick his whole life, never doing shit with shit, and I'm thinking to myself "fuck man . . .—"
>
> (90)

I do not mean to suggest that precariousness invites indifference to fine gradations of urban geography. Those forced to eke out a precarious existence within the city are, if anything, *more* likely to be aware of such gradations. And yet, this is the Teenage Boy's longest speech—indeed, this is the longest speech *in the entire play*, uttered by a character who had previously spoken only sparely (38). Property concerns become the most universal shared value in the play. Imogen Tyler describes contemporary London property relations as "producing some subjects as successful citizens and others as variously precarious or failed" (62). *Boy* inadvertently goes further, suggesting that it is concerns over property that makes subjects intelligible at all. The Boy, bereft not only of such geographic self-awareness—but also of the aspirations it reveals—has nothing to say.

We Want What You Have addresses this almost ontological prevalence of the theme of property ownership on the London stage during the Brexit interregnum. I show how private property's hold on the contemporary theatrical imagination, its influence over onstage plots and production aesthetics, has come at the expense of the irresolute, the uncertain, the unusual, the inchoate, and the exploratory. Geographically, I describe how the neighbourhoods in which a variety of London theatres sit have been transformed in the past 10–15 years by international wealth flowing into the city. This increase in prices has extended property anxiety upward. The resulting anxiety has narrowed sympathy for the experiences of other sorts of people: has made what gets staged focus on an ever-more-narrow range of characters and settings, while also implying that this narrow range has universal significance. Property ownership thereby anchors what Beverley Skeggs terms a "powerful" class perspective: one that "eclipse[s] all other perspectives to ensure they are the only ones which can be taken."[35]

To secure this perspective among their audiences, the productions I read often alternate realist scenes with moments of interrupted reality: frequently, through dance-like sequences in which characters move around in ways that heighten or exaggerate everyday activities. Yet rather than invite alternative perspectives on contemporary society, interrupted motion in these performances only foreclosed its becoming or remaining the way that it was. These performances were all critical-seeming, each in their way addressing social issues: migration in the wake of the Arab Spring, life as a transgender person, the difficulties of female infertility, and (looming in the background) the ongoing housing crisis. Yet they all remained fixated on the private ownership of property—locking audiences into the way things are, rather than inviting them to speculate on how they might be.[36]

My study defines private home ownership, or the aspiration to own a home, as too often what separated the representable from the unrepresentable in London theatre. Choosing property ownership as the central arena of contemporary concerns forecloses sympathies with others—particularly, with those outside of the so-called London Bubble, the intensely inward-looking monoculture that the city sustains in both popular myth and (frequently) observable reality. Anxious times made local audiences less willing to consider perspectives beyond their own. They are nudged along by a global audience hungry for a very traditional kind of Englishness: one based on the familiar offerings of the heritage industries, focused on the experiences of the bourgeois classes or better.[37] Tim Butler and Chris Hamnett conclude their 2011 study of London housing with the question: "We have shown that the middle classes are not able to satisfy their long-term needs; where, then, does this leave other groups who are even more in need?"[38] On this London stage the answer was, frequently, nowhere.

The selectiveness of property vision is particularly pertinent to contemporary re-imaginings of classical plays. In such updatings, the ostensibly universal or at least potentially different truths found in historical plays are given local reassignments. Presented slightly before the Brexit referendum, a 2015 Almeida Theatre production of *Medea*, in a new version by the novelist Rachel Cusk, situated the story within a world like the affluent part of the theatre's neighbourhood. Euripides' Medea murders her children after taking a new wife. Cusk dismisses the verisimilitude of this kind of narrative for contemporary society: "I guess there are a couple of women on the planet who murder their children," she notes in an interview, "but these days we see that as psychotic behaviour, those people are mentally ill, they suffer a great deal and they don't kill their children for the reasons Medea kills her children. What I want is for people to think, 'Here are some things I recognise, little echoes of my own experience.' Medea has everything to do with lots of people's lives and I couldn't write a play in a modern setting about a woman who kills her children."[39]

What constitutes this "lots of people" and "modern setting" reveals the presumption of a middle-class audience that Beswick diagnoses. The play never leaves what the stage directions term "A middle class, vaguely bohemian domestic space."[40] There's even the "sofa" that Burkhoff predicted (9). This house's sale figures prominently in the plot, Medea removing it from the market as a retaliatory measure to her husband's remarriage. (This, and attacking him online, become this play's reconfiguring of Euripides' murder.) The main character and the staging reflect similar beliefs, as the domestic interior and what occurs within it expand to incorporate seemingly the whole of the world. Of the end of her marriage, she states, "What kind of love is it that needs the whole world to disappear before it can exist? *Pause.* That isn't love. It's genocide" (26). Nothing on the stage pushes back against this statement. A genocide is an act of violence against a wide population, yet the play's world is limited. (The one non-middle-class character is listed as a Cleaner.)

Culturally influential cities like New York and London can succumb to this particular sort of provincialism. Their cultural lives are deep and intricate enough that they do not necessarily need to look elsewhere for influences. Indeed this intricacy can hide internal multiplicities. The Cusk *Medea* made the problems of divorce in an affluent area retroactively colonise the strangeness of the Greek original. But many other London plays had a difficult time breaking out of the Bubble. Part of the "unravelling of an imagined community" that O'Toole describes is exactly this: an unwillingness on the part of art makers to show audiences the unfamiliar, or to question the default assumptions present in a particular area. An assumed audience's values in one particular place at one particular moment are treated as inescapable, with shock triggering anxieties leading to a retreat from a more general sympathy. All books are, for their writers, akin to therapy. These were also my anxieties—I write, in what follows, about the ways I felt my own sympathies being manipulated and limited. Parallel projects might track the architectonics of shock, anxiety, and restricted sympathy rippling across the nation's regional theatres. My focus here, however, is the particular conditions of theatre and theatregoing in London.

3 Subsidised privacy: an aesthetic theory of the arts council

How did we wind up here? There are, of course, the grim facts of contemporary housing reality. Getting and sustaining a private residence and an education for one's children in London has become an expensive and difficult task—particularly given the state's increasing absentia from these spheres. You can choose what apocalyptical difficult-of-living facts you like. The cost of home ownership, for example, rose by 259% in the 20 years between 1997 and 2017, with real wages increasing 68%.[41] Everyone slides down a peg in terms of the accommodations they are able to afford. Something analogous occurs with qualifications:

> The guarantees offered by academic qualifications, which nevertheless still afford good insurance against unemployment, were likewise called into question when it was observed that, with equivalent qualifications, the young invariably accede to positions inferior to those of their elders at the same age.[42]

The contracting of opportunities for the previously comfortable middle classes, coupled with the pernicious effects of survey culture, has made a limited range of classes representable as an entire world. And a key focus of these classes' anxiety is private ownership, particularly of the home.

I also believe that contemporary arts policy has nudged theatre-makers in these representation directions—has incentivised theatre-makers to stoke and solidify these anxieties, rather than to offer perspective on them.

The stories the UK tells about itself are often collective ones. The Somme, the Blitz, and the creation of the National Health Service (NHS) can all be framed as moments of national cohesion, and usually are. In contrast, the governments the country votes into power favour privatisation. The arts environment in present-day London reflects the necessary contradictions between these two positions. The theatre industry is, on the one hand, government-subsidised in a variety of ways, from the training of actors to the funding of individual companies. On the other hand, it is encouraged to address its audiences as consumers encouraged to think of their arts experience only in *momentary* terms, and to feel what I term *resonant ownership* over these experiences, to see them as something that they possess privately.[43] And this ownership paradigm features prominently in recent guidelines published by the Arts Council UK, particularly around the practice of data collection. The Arts Council does not fund all of the theatre that occurs in London. But it remains aspirationally open to all theatre companies, and, crucially, funding is important to companies seeking to have a long institutional life.[44]

Many of most significant directors and writers working in London at the moment work within a similar paradigm concerning the mixture of public and private. The playwright and director Simon Stone, for example, whose *Yerma* I read in my sixth chapter, responds to critics of his radical adaptations of plays: "They say: 'He wants to reduce theatre to HBO.' My first thought is: Jesus Christ, if theatre could be half as good as HBO, we'd be hitting gold."[45] To be alive right now in much of the world is to be aware of HBO's programming, particularly the fantasy epic *Game of Thrones* (2011–19). HBO offers its programming as an expensive upper tier of cable television. It also receives UK state funding, for example tax breaks for filming in Northern Ireland.[46] *Game of Thrones*, then, is a publicly funded television programme accessible only to private audiences: an ethos of public-private partnerships, with the state in effect funding some individuals' consumer choices.

Consumer choice has gone hand in hand with arts organisations' forced embrace of audience data collection, as the government has encouraged these organisations to track consumer preferences via quantitative surveys. "Great Art and Culture for Everyone," the Arts Council's current planning document, lays out a plan by which the Council will "support the arts and cultural sector to develop a set of national quality measures and integrate these within a programme of self-evaluation."[47] This commitment is sustained, undiminished, in the currently circulating draft of the 2020–30 plan.[48] Getting funded requires obtaining "measures": quantifiable data, which comes from surveying "the views of audiences, users and peers."[49]

The Council instructs organisations to ask "How well do you serve your regular audiences, participants, clients, funders or community?"[50] This question is in line with the Council's stated belief that, particularly in a time of restricted budgets, the arts sector is meant to assume an essentially governmental role "in local regeneration, in attracting tourists, in the development of talent and innovation, in improving health and well-being, and in delivering essential services."[51] A role in "essential services" cannot be exploratory or experimental, any more than an ambulance service might be; the "regular audiences" of a theatre in an affluent area are most probably affluent people, as are those who travel to London to see it.[52] This also directly opposes certain sorts of artistic autonomy, making it harder to ask questions that might only address a minority of a community, or even to speak beyond the limits of what "regular audiences, participants, clients, funders" might allow.

The way to substantiate the responses to these questions is through data collection—a practice of privatisation on several levels. Most basically, the Arts Council hires private companies to run their data surveys.[53] But consumer data surveys would reflect privatisation even if they were conducted by governments themselves. In theory, anyone can participate in a consumer survey. In practice, the means to complete a survey, from Internet access to the time to do so, requires private resources.

Moreover, surveys by their nature address individual preferences. Surveys do not ask whether the museum or play we attended was good for society. Audiences are instead asked their immediate impressions of an artwork; we are asked to assume individual ownership of the things that we watch, and the art that we support. For the purpose of the survey there is, as it were, no such thing as a society—there are individuals, and occasionally their families. In terms of the arts, this sort of survey skews conservative—not necessarily politically, but aesthetically. Something aesthetically challenging seeks to push back against norms; surveys seek to reflect them ("reflecting the population," in the words of the Council).[54] To reflect does not necessarily mean to change. The Council's "Quality Metrics" for assessment within the arts sector read as follows:

Concept: it was an interesting idea
Presentation: it was well produced and presented
Distinctiveness: it was different from things I've experienced before
Challenge: it was thought-provoking
Captivation: it was absorbing and held my attention
Enthusiasm: I would come to something like this again
Local impact: it is important that it's happening here
Relevance: it has something to say about the world in which we live
Rigour: it was well thought through and put together[55]

These criteria value cohesiveness and unity over diffusiveness: "an interesting idea" that is "well produced and presented." On a certain level this would seem hard to argue with. Yet I am struck by how little resistance to the present moment the artwork is allowed to offer: how the work of art must appear as a single, self-sufficient, absorbing, individual action. There are a variety of other ways to think about artworks more diffusively. So, there is diffusion in time, for artworks that take time to pay off. Equally, something that is difficult—something that may not make someone write, immediately, that "I would come to something like this again"—seems precluded by these criteria.

Subsidised art in an age of austerity can wind up supporting what is already surviving: something that has found an established niche, playing to an entrenched audience's expectations. The Council cites as a particular success "the career of a folk artist like Sam Carter," which "has flourished and his talent—and ingenuity with difficult tunings—has grown." Would Carter's tunings have been less ingenious in a more favourable economic climate? Perhaps it was a desire to stand out—to compete and win—that led Carter to innovate. But I have always understood the process of art-making as a conversation with something vaguer, and more mysterious: what Derek Attridge describes as "trying to verbalize a cluster of interconnected ideas that I can only dimly apprehend," as "nebulous outlines take shape as phrases."[56] Audience data has a hard time inviting the nebulous into being. We don't entirely know why we make art—*Roots* didn't entirely know how to end Beatie's story. What Attridge describes depends on something unconscious and vague, rather than in the concrete facts of the social playing-field.

These recommendations do not promote art that would help us think outside of the present moment. The survey that the Council recommends asks audiences to consider something as a one-off: whether the individual performance was "absorbing" that presented an "interesting idea." As Roger Tomlinson writes,

valuing art based primarily on the experiences it produces, in fact devalues the work itself . . . post-event surveys primarily measure the 'experienced impacts', perhaps within a day or so, and ignore the 'extended impacts', probably weeks or even years later).[57]

This emphasis on the short term gives less space for the slow, collective work of addressing social inequalities or problems. It is the time of extended impact that might allow new communities to form around the experience of artworks. An initial survey, after all, does not give us time to talk over what we have seen with other people. Emphasising the momentary in this way limits art's ability to propose, much less enact, meaningful social change. It is what it is.

3 Terms of argument

Four patterns reappeared throughout these performances: what I will term *mimetic irony, exhausted radicalism and the hedonistic body, class capture*, and *resonant ownership*. Each reflects a withdrawal from a belief in political or social improvement achieved by individuals acting together: from collective action or experience. The first of these terms, *mimetic irony*, describes the tendency of humour to offer verisimilitude—the confirmation of something that seems realistic—rather than any independent perspective on, or critique of, that realism.[58] Humour is part of London theatre's echo chamber, a tool of its embubblement: something that encloses these characters, rather than offers them a perspective on or escape from this enclosure. So, *Yerma's* bantering marrieds spend the first third of the play being politically incorrect to one another, mocking homosexuals and the disabled; and the last third playing out a tragedy premised on a very traditional understanding of procreation and biological gender roles. For the characters onstage, humour does not offer the possibility of an alternate perspective. Rather, it confirms the rounded humanity of the character who is funny, while making what happens to them seem inevitable. Reflecting the nation's status in its own and the world's imagination, being funny has become what is simply expected of British people; this expectation has usurped the space of critique and the possibility of improvement that critique promises.

Also running through these plays is what I term *exhausted radicalism and the hedonistic body*. Most of these plays make sex something to be sought after for private hedonism, rather than a right established collectively for communal benefit. For a concise definition of what this means, I point towards something written by Meghan Vaughan, one of the best current British theatre bloggers, in a review of a 2018 stage remounting of *Jubilee*, a Derek Jarman film from 1978:

> Well, we shrug, if the world's fucked we may as well party . . . Maybe I'm kidding myself to think that there is anything more to strive for than a decent Saturday night, some good sex, and friendship. Maybe embracing that is the radical thing.[59]

This is a response to an age of anxiety, to the exhaustion of this late moment of sustained austerity: a turn away from collective politics and towards a kind of de facto privatisation.

Apolitical hedonism goes hand in hand with what I term *class capture*, in which the concerns of one local class are assigned a distortive universality. Class capture is the product of focused anxiety. The lives of the comfortable classes can seem precarious enough that they constitute an *agon* unto themselves: so, the Medea myth becomes the story of people living in a middle-class house. This situation reflects a wider tendency in British society, wherein the still-formidable resources of the state have been directed increasingly towards those able to afford a certain level of buy-in. Council-run athletic centres charge membership fees; universities both are extensively funded and require ever-increasing student fees; NHS care is managed by a range of subsidised private providers. And state-supported art begins to represent the entire world in terms of the interests of an affluent local class increasingly transitioning into a global one. Two of the theatres I write about, the Arts Theatre in Soho and the King's Head in Islington, will almost certainly no longer exist in the same form by the time you read this, having become part of new developments aimed at affluent foreigners. By *resonant ownership*, I refer to the ways that this preference for the privately owned over the publicly funded influences the way things look, and the way they are framed, in theatres, art galleries, and other spaces primarily devoted to what used to be called "high" culture. I want to examine the ways that the imaginative horizon—the boundaries of what we can think about on stage—has been captured by the interests of the property-owning classes. Reflecting, in the words of the Arts Council, the lives of its audiences has come to mean reflecting the lives of the sorts of people best-equipped to fill in arts surveys.

4 Chapter summary

This is an inquiry into the London stage's tendency to be what Berkhoff accuses it of being: reflective rather than imaginative; reproductive of extant class conditions rather than critical or transformative of them. It describes this as a mindset particular to para-Brexit London; and, in its conclusion, offers readers the possibility of offering structured feedback against this mindset.

My first two chapters address London's relation to its recent past: to a time of greater openness in terms of both politics and property. "Typical Girls: or, the Privately-owned Punk Squat," describes *Fran and Leni* (2015) by Sadie Hasler, seen at the King's Head Theatre in Islington in 2016. This chapter shows how property and class inflect how we imagine the past. The play twins a story about the fight for the wider acknowledgement of female experience in the punk movement with one of property ownership and the establishment of the private household. I link this to the fate of the King's Head itself. An agit-prop venue in the 1970s, the theatre itself will soon move into a private property development aimed at international investors. I show how narratives of privatisation now rewrite the country's radical past.

My second chapter, "Brexit's Dispossessed," addresses property, nationalism, and Brexit via *My Country: A Work in Progress* (2017) and *Boudica* (2017). *My Country* was first presented in Southwark and then toured around the country. I show how these anxieties about London's housing market take place within a broader national conversation regarding private ownership and citizenship—a conversation taken up with renewed force after Brexit. In the piece, personified regions of the country meet to give voice to their constituents, who describe their reasons for voting the way they did. *My Country* examines the deep economic unease that runs through the country, where the private ownership of land sustains deep structural inequalities. Comprised of verbatim interviews with people throughout the country, it reveals the Brexit decision as a response to a dissatisfaction that unequal property ownership only exacerbated. The self-conscious decision to not interview London's residents—to get outside of the bubble—only deepened the sense that London was something atypical of the country: a world city, and so an exception, rather than part of England. I argue that this absence shocked London audiences out of sympathy with the rest of the country, emphasising the present moment as a competition of worldviews rather than a conversation. *Boudica*, also presented in Southwark at Shakespeare's Globe, reflected similar anxieties in its reactivation of a figure from English mythic history. The EU became rapacious Romans, and hybrid citizenship was only offered to the native-born. Around domestic legend, attitudes towards foreigners hardened.

The next two chapters examine the relationship between generations: the established Baby Boomers, now well into retirement, and the rising Millennials, fighting for a reduced place in the austerity-defined world the Boomers left behind. "Transnationalism" reads *Rotterdam* (2015), performed at the Arts Theatre in Soho in 2017, as a play about Millennial self-determination. Addressing one half of a lesbian couple's gender transition, the play addresses more generally young adults' struggles to find meaningful work and life options. Rotterdam, a port city, becomes a reflection of the characters' own liminal stage in their lives. Millennial self-determination comes at the expense of meaningful integration with Europe, and within a post-privatisation mindset. The freedom the couple are given to determine their relationships and identities is not supported by the state: they must do these things entirely on their own. Meanwhile the Arts Theatre—the site of the first English production of *Waiting for Godot*, among other landmarks in theatre history—is converted into a luxury hotel aimed at the international market, facilitating transient experiences of the city for tourists over the long-standing development of a cultural product for residents.

My fourth chapter, conversely, addresses the London housing market that awaits young people. "Village Feel" addresses two plays at venues in Swiss Cottage, a North London neighbourhood that has been battling—with great success—to hinder the development of new housing. *Deposit* (2015, 2017), at the Hampstead Theatre's Downstairs space, addresses young Londoners attempting to move onto the so-called property ladder by living together in a cramped one-bedroom apartment. *The Devils* (1961), at the Royal Central School of Speech and Drama, describes Satan worship in a medieval French town. Seemingly these performances have little in common. Yet in both, young people fought the same battles as their parents' generation, only without the subsidies that generation received. I show how housing is a tool of control by the old over the young. Collectively these plays show a generation that has received various freedoms from the 1960s but not the space to practice them in.

The last two chapters address the desirability of London's property within the world economy: for those who live here already, and for those who struggle to stay. I firstly look at property's influence over how we imagine migration. In "Croydon versus the World," I show how a festival dedicated to the Iranian playwright Nassim Soleimanpour at the Bush Theatre in Shepherd's Bush revealed and stimulated the anxieties of London theatregoers. Soleimanpour's work in performance provides an opportunity to reflect on property and migration. Soleimanpour's semi-improved plays, *Blank* (2015) and *White Rabbit Red Rabbit* (2011), provide a performance scaffolding whose opportunities for local detail are sketched in by local performers. One young volunteer drawn from the audience gave a clear articulation of Millennial values: pleased with new sexual freedoms, but frustrated with lack of career progression and—most significantly—unable to imagine any sort of collective remedy to these issues. She had a three-way, and it changed her life, but she can't imagine a state-supported retirement. I read Soleimanpour as a cannily ingratiating playwright, whose plays adapt themselves to the conceptual limitations of the stages on which they appear—in particular, their fixation on private households and property ownership. I consider what it means to advance a vision of the migrant as a state-unsupported entrepreneur in light of the nearby Grenfell Tower fires.

My sixth chapter, "*Yerma* on the Internet," addresses property and the female body. Simon Stone's adaptation of *Yerma* (2015) was an international sensation, with particular acclaim given to Billie Piper's performance in the title role. A middle-class couple buys a house and then sees their marriage unravel over unsuccessful fertility treatments. I show how this play makes its image of middle-class London life, absent the presence of other classes, into a global commodity. The title character's unravelling over her inability to have a child takes place in a world in which both a functional "pelvic floor" and a home conversion are the source of international scrutiny and envy.[60] Reflecting this age of "we want what you have," the production was simulcast around the world, and has subsequently travelled to New York. Seeing the simulcast of the play at the Arthouse, a chain independent cinema in the North London neighbourhood of Crouch End, I observed London having its fantasy life reflected back at itself at second hand—indeed, as one of the many people who could not get tickets to the live production.

My conclusion suggests a remedy to this relentless focus on property, suggesting strategies for audiences to take command of data-driven surveys. I use a reading of Nina Raine's *Consent* (2018) to offer audiences a checklist for demanding better theatre. Through Raine's play, a legal drama about a rape trial, I break down the way that non-middle-class subjects—like the play's central victim—are elided from theatrical debates about important subjects. Our present moment truly is, for better and for worse, a moment when audience feedback can make a difference to what gets put on in the theatre. While anticipating a future in which audience feedback will form a less significant part of what theatres are forced to consider, my conclusion also tells audiences in the present how to offer the kind of feedback that will lead to broader-minded, inclusive, and transformative theatre.

Finally, in my afterword, I consider a longer history of property relations in recent English theatre, reaching back to Jez Butterworth's *Jerusalem* (2009) to locate it as a last gasp for certain values of collective citizenship rather than its privately owned alternatives. I read how quickly *Jerusalem's* queasily evocative commons-dweller is replaced by the effectively feudal landowner of Mike Bartlett's *Albion* (2017), a play whose 2020 West End revival was one of the last major productions mounted before the Coronavirus lockdown put a temporary end to this era of theatre and theatre-going. I look in closing at Ambreen Razia's *The Diary of a Hounslow Girl* (2015), a single-artist piece, as a possible alternative to this relentless property conformism: a recent play holding open the hope for the future that Beatie Bryant represented.

Notes

1 John Lanchester, *Capital* (London: Faber, 2012), 18.
2 "I was in Edinburgh a couple of weeks ago, and from looking in estate agents' windows it was apparent that I could swap our unremarkable south London house for a castle. This isn't a figure of speech: I actually could buy a Scottish castle." ("London's House Price Madness Just Goes On and On," *The Evening Standard* (London), September 8, 2014).
3 Chris Hamnett, *Unequal City: London in the Global Arena* (London: Routledge, 2003).
4 David Harvey, *A Brief History of Neoliberalism* (Oxford: Oxford University Press, 2005), 7. Harvey defines the term as "a theory of political economic practices that proposes that human well-being can best be advanced by liberating individual entrepreneurial freedoms and skills within an institutional framework characterized by strong private property rights" in a trinity that also includes "free markets, and free trade" (2).
5 Anita Biressi and Heather Nunn, *Class and Contemporary British Culture* (Basingstoke: Palgrave Macmillan, 2013), 8.
6 Arnold Wesker, *Roots* (London: Bloomsbury Methuen Drama, 2018).
7 Ibid.
8 Dan Rebellato, *1956 and All That* (London: Routledge, 1999), 20.
9 Eve Sedgwick, *Tendencies* (London: Routledge, 1993), 8.
10 Katie Beswick, *Social Housing in Performance* (London: Methuen, 2019), 5.
11 While Jen Harvie's 2013 study of art under neoliberalism surveys "social engagement and fair, democratic opportunity" occurring in what she terms "socially turned art and performance" in a variety of venues, this study addresses the inverse: the moments where performances in London turned away from a broad account of society, choosing instead to focus on issues relating to private property ownership. Jen Harvie, *Fair Play* (Houndsmills: Palgrave Macmillan, 2013), 2, 5.
12 Harvey, *A Brief History of Neoliberalism*, 181.
13 Philip Ridley, *Radiant Vermin* (London: Methuen, 2015), 5, 115. I would like to thank an anonymous reviewer for bringing this play to my attention. Bristol, too, has been immensely impacted by London housing prices, its own house values having been driven up by those leaving the city.
14 Beswick, *Social Housing in Performance*, 98.
15 BOP Consulting and Graham Devlin Associates, *Analysis of Theatre in England* (London: BOP Consulting and Graham Devlin Associates, 2016), 39.

16 "SPID Theatre Company," https://spidtheatre.com/.
17 Beswick, *Social Housing in Performance*, 103.
18 I am indebted in this regard to the description and practice of the concept throughout Beswick, *Social Housing in Performance*.
19 Hamnett, *Unequal City*, 10.
20 Ibid, 24.
21 It is, of course, impossible to comprehensively survey all of the theatre going on in the city in a particular time period. Examples that would run contrary to this account are eminently imaginable. The Battersea Arts Centre, a community theatre space and arts incubator in South London, devoted its 2019 Homegrown Festival—a program of new work—to the theme of "Occupy," devoting itself to how people lived (or failed to do so) within the society. As part of this festival, the future dystopian *High Rise eState of Mind* (2019) reminded audiences that precarity is possible for homeowners as well, showing among other characters a nurse still needing to work well past retirement age to afford a mortgage. SPID Theatre's *The Burning Tower* (2019), which I saw in an actual tower block estate at Kensal House near the site of the Grenfell tragedy, reminded audiences of how the 1980s' Right to Buy policy had divided working-class communities, creating in effect an inheritance of which families could remain in their communities and which would be forced to go. I note that these venues are out-of-the-way places, with smaller audiences, than the venues I focus on. My claim is not so much to totality as to a prominent trend—albeit one that, in this theatregoer's admittedly partial view, began to seem overwhelming.
22 Fintan O'Toole, "It Was Never about Europe. Brexit Is Britain's Reckoning with Itself," *The Guardian* (London), January 18, 2019, www.theguardian.com/commentisfree/2019/jan/18/europe-brexit-britain-state-politics-fit-for-purpose.
23 James Rosbrook-Thompson and Gary Armstrong note how importantly "skilled manual workers" were to the initial popularity of right-to-buy and indeed the Conservative governments who promoted it (*Mixed-Occupancy Housing in London: A Living Tapestry* [London: Palgrave Macmillan, 2018], 31.) This narrative is a thorny one: many of these buyers were incentivised to resell to property developers, receiving only an initial payoff rather than a long-term stake in the value of their property.
24 Chris Hamnett, for example, notes that "gentrifiers comprise a specific fraction of the professional and managerial middle classes, distinguished by high levels of education and a strong representation in the liberal arts . . . they . . . tend to be more to the left politically than the middle classes as a whole, who are generally more Conservative voting." Hamnett, *Unequal City*, 153.
25 BOP Consulting and Graham Devlin Associates, *Analysis of Theatre in England*, 16.
26 Michael Billington, *State of the Nation: British Theatre since 1945* (London: Faber, 2007), 7.
27 Steven Berkhoff, interview by Geoff Colman, National Theatre, October 2, 2017.
28 Susannah Clapp, "Bertie Carvel Is Unmissable as Rupert Murdoch, Review of Ink," *The Observer* (London), Sunday, July 2, 2017.
29 James Graham, *Ink* (London: Methuen, 2017).
30 Ibid, 130.
31 See Lauren Berlant, *Cruel Optimism* (Durham, NC: Duke University Press, 2011), 204.
32 Thirty-eight percent of its children live in poverty, for example, and it rates well above the city average for its poverty rate and, critically, its housing affordability. Trust for London, "Islington," February 15, 2019, www.trustforlondon.org.uk/data/boroughs/islington-poverty-and-inequality-indicators/.
33 Almeida Theatre, "Boy Production Page," *Boy*, 2016, https://almeida.co.uk/whats-on/boy/5-apr-2016-28-may-2016.
34 Leo Butler, *Boy* (London: Bloomsbury Methuen Drama, 2016), 120. All subsequent citations are provided parenthetically by page number.

35 Beverley Skeggs, *Class, Self, Culture* (London: Routledge, 2004), 6.

36 My thinking on this has been influenced by Jacques Rancière's idea of the "division of the sensible": the way that a particular political order will set up the total of what is representable at a particular moment for a particular society. See *The Politics of Aesthetics*, trans. Gabriel Rockhill (London: Continuum, 2004), 3 and passim.

37 The notion of theatre's class exclusions has a long critical history—see, for example, John McGrath, *A Good Night Out* (London: Eyre Methuen, 1981). It has also been the subject of ongoing reports from government and arts agencies—see, for example, the *Acting Up Report: Labour's Inquiry into Access and Diversity in the Performing Arts* (London: The Labour Party, 2017). This history, and resulting programs to address it, have had a tendency to run face-first into the ostensibly objective metrics of saleability. By definition, something that interrupts normal patterns of cultural consumption is not going to be popular; if it were, it would be selling in the first place. "Britishness" in recent years has had a worrying tendency to be recapitulated via high-bourgeois forms, into which alternatively classed people are in effect invited in to participate as at best visitors to their own country's culture. Lucy Potter and Claire Westall describe how a particular bourgeois tradition reinforces the marketing of a particular sort of middle-class subject. ("Neoliberal Britain's Austerity Foodscape," *New Formations* 80–81 (2013): 158–59.) It's this *Great British Bakeoff* version of England that sells well overseas, for example to American audiences: one of well-appointed interiors and middle-class quirkiness. Ben Brantley, the *New York Times* theatre reviewer most often assigned articles on London during the time this book was being written, is arguably one of the most significant theatre reviewers in the city: what he recommends tends to sell. And what Brantley chooses to observe—to use his own words—is often "offerings . . . unlikely to disconcert habitual watchers of 'Masterpiece' television." (Ben Brantley, "On London Stages, Britain Considers Its Divided Soul," *The New York Times*, November 13, 2017, https://nyti.ms/2jom9v6).

38 Tim Butler and Chris Hamnett, *Ethnicity, Class and Aspiration: Understanding London's New East End* (Bristol: Policy, 2011), 244.

39 Susanna Rustin, "Rachel Cusk Interview," *The Guardian* (London), October 3, 2015, www.theguardian.com/books/2015/oct/03/rachel-cusk-interview-medea-divorce-almeida-theatre-london-feminist-euripides.

40 Rachel Cusk, *Medea* (London: Oberon Books, 2015), 9. All subsequent citations are by page number.

41 "UK House Prices 'Least Affordable Ever'," *The Financial Times* (London), March 17, 2017, www.ft.com/content/ea8f28fc-0b08-11e7-ac5a-903b21361b43.

42 Luc Boltanski and Eve Chiapello, *The New Spirit of Capitalism* (London: Verso, 2007), xli.

43 "Ownership" is, for example, one of the Seven Quality Principles established for arts organisations working with children. Arts Council England, "Quality Principles," 2018, www.artscouncil.org.uk/quality-metrics/quality-principles.

44 See, for example, Brian Cook, "Shocking the System: The Arts Council, the British Council, and the Paradox of Cherub Theatre Company," *Theatre History Studies* 35 (2016): 73.

45 Nancy Groves, "Simon Stone: 'If Theatre Could Be Half as Good as HBO, We'd Be Hitting Gold'," *The Guardian* (London), 2016, www.theguardian.com/stage/2016/jun/03/simon-stone-theatre-film-the-daughter-yerma.

46 "Game of Thrones Brings Estimated £150m to Northern Ireland," *BBC*, July 11, 2016, www.bbc.co.uk/news/uk-northern-ireland-36749938.

47 Arts Council England, "Great Art and Culture for Everyone," 2013, 60, www.artscouncil.org.uk/sites/default/files/download-file/Great%20art%20and%20culture%20for%20everyone.pdf.

48 "In all of this work, Arts Council England will use data to build and share a more sophisticated picture of investment at a local level." Arts Council UK, "Draft Strategy 2020–2030," 2019, 13, www.artscouncil.org.uk/sites/default/files/download-file/Draft_Strategy_summer_consultation_2019.pdf.
49 Arts Council England, "Great Art and Culture for Everyone," 44.
50 Arts Council UK, "Self-Evaluation Toolkit," 2019, www.artscouncil.org.uk/self-evaluation-toolkit. I accessed this web page in September of 2018.
51 Arts Council England, "Great Art and Culture for Everyone," 14.
52 BOP Consulting and Graham Devlin Associates, *Analysis of Theatre in England,* 16.
53 "In September 2015 Arts Council England gave a grant of £300,000 to Counting What Counts Ltd, to support a diverse range of 150 National Portfolio Organisations and Major Partner Museums to test the Quality Metrics evaluation framework across three events" (Arts Council England, "Quality Metrics Q&A," Undated, 3, www.artscouncil.org.uk/sites/default/files/download-file/Quality%20Metrics%20Q%26A%20FINAL.pdf).
54 Arts Council England, "Great Art and Culture for Everyone," 6.
55 "Self-Evaluation Toolkit," web page.
56 Derek Attridge, "Innovation, Literature, Ethics: Relating to the Other," *PMLA* 114, no. 1 (1999): 20.
57 Roger Tomlinson, "What Are We Counting?" *Arts Professional* (Magazine), May 25, 2017, www.artsprofessional.co.uk/magazine/article/what-are-we-counting.
58 Thanks to Julia Ng for this term.
59 Meghan Vaghaun, "Jubille," *Synonyms for Churlish* (blog), *Medium.com,* March 13, 2018, https://synonymsforchurlish.com/jubilee-chris-goode-royal-exchange-38d52b192108.
60 Simon Stone, *Yerma* (London: Oberon Books, 2017), 61.

Works cited

Almeida Theatre. "Boy, Production Page." *Boy.* 2016. https://almeida.co.uk/whats-on/boy/5-apr-2016-28-may-2016.

Arts Council England. "Great Art and Culture for Everyone." 2013. www.artscouncil.org.uk/sites/default/files/download-file/Great%20art%20and%20culture%20for%20everyone.pdf.

———. "Quality Principles." 2018. www.artscouncil.org.uk/quality-metrics/quality-principles.

———. "Draft Strategy 2020–2030." 2019. www.artscouncil.org.uk/sites/default/files/download-file/Draft_Strategy_summer_consultation_2019.pdf.

———. "Self-Evaluation Toolkit." 2019. www.artscouncil.org.uk/self-evaluation-toolkit.

———. "Quality Metrics Q&A." Undated. www.artscouncil.org.uk/sites/default/files/download-file/Quality%20Metrics%20Q%26A%20FINAL.pdf.

Attridge, Derek. "Innovation, Literature, Ethics: Relating to the Other." *PMLA* 114, no. 1 (1999): 20–1.

Berkhoff, Steven. Interviewed by Geoff Colman, National Theatre, October 2, 2017.

Beswick, Katie. *Social Housing in Performance.* London: Methuen, 2019.

Billington, Michael. *State of the Nation: British Theatre since 1945.* London: Faber, 2007.

Biressi, Anita, and Heather Nunn. *Class and Contemporary British Culture.* Basingstoke: Palgrave Macmillan, 2013.

Boltanski, Luc, and Eve Chiapello. *The New Spirit of Capitalism.* London: Verso, 2007.

BOP Consulting and Graham Devlin Associates. *Analysis of Theatre in England.* London: BOP Consulting and Graham Devlin Associates, 2016.

Brantley, Ben. "On London Stages, Britain Considers Its Divided Soul." *The New York Times*, November 13, 2017. https://nyti.ms/2jom9v6.

Butler, Leo. *Boy*. London: Bloomsbury, 2016.

Butler, Tim, and Chris Hamnett. *Ethnicity, Class and Aspiration: Understanding London's New East End*. Bristol: Policy, 2011.

Clapp, Susannah. "Bertie Carvel Is Unmissable as Rupert Murdoch Review of *Ink*, by James Graham." *The Observer* (London), Sunday, July 2, 2017.

Cook, Brian. "Shocking the System: The Arts Council, the British Council, and the Paradox of Cherub Theatre Company." *Theatre History Studies* 35 (2016): 73–94.

Cusk, Rachel. *Medea*. London: Oberon Books, 2015.

Girvin, Sara. "Game of Thrones Brings Estimated £150m to Northern Ireland." *BBC*, July 11, 2016. www.bbc.co.uk/news/uk-northern-ireland-36749938.

Graham, James. *Ink*. London: Methuen, 2017.

Groves, Nancy. "Simon Stone: 'If Theatre Could Be Half as Good as HBO, We'd Be Hitting Gold'." *The Guardian* (London), June 3, 2016. www.theguardian.com/stage/2016/jun/03/simon-stone-theatre-film-the-daughter-yerma.

Hamnett, Chris. *Unequal City: London in the Global Arena*. London: Routledge, 2003.

Harvey, David. *A Brief History of Neoliberalism*. Oxford: Oxford University Press, 2005.

Harvie, Jen. *Fair Play: Art, Performance and Neoliberalism*. Houndsmills: Palgrave Macmillan, 2013.

Lanchester, John. *Capital*. London: Faber, 2012.

———. "London's House Price Madness Just Goes On and On." *The Evening Standard* (London), September 8, 2014.

McGrath, John. *A Good Night Out*. London: Eyre Methuen, 1981.

O'Toole, Fintan. "It Was Never about Europe. Brexit Is Britain's Reckoning with Itself." *The Guardian* (London), January 18, 2019. www.theguardian.com/commentisfree/2019/jan/18/europe-brexit-britain-state-politics-fit-for-purpose.

Potter, Lucy, and Claire Westall. "Neoliberal Britain's Austerity Foodscape." *New Formations* 80–81 (2013): 155–78.

Rancière, Jacques. *The Politics of Aesthetics: The Distribution of the Sensible*. Translated by Gabriel Rockhill. London: Continuum, 2004.

Rebellato, Dan. *1956 and All That*. London: Routledge, 1999.

Ridley, Philip. *Radiant Vermin*. London: Methuen, 2015.

Rosbrook-Thompson, James, and Gary Armstrong. *Mixed-Occupancy Housing in London: A Living Tapestry*. London: Palgrave Macmillan, 2018.

Rush, Kayla. *Acting up Report: Labour's Inquiry into Access and Diversity in the Performing Arts*. London: The Labour Party, 2017.

Rustin, Susanna. "Rachel Cusk Interview." *The Guardian* (London), October 3, 2015. www.theguardian.com/books/2015/oct/03/rachel-cusk-interview-medea-divorce-almeida-theatre-london-feminist-euripides.

Sedgwick, Eve. *Tendencies*. London: Routledge, 1993.

Skeggs, Beverley. *Class, Self, Culture*. London: Routledge, 2004.

"SPID Theatre Company." *SPID Theatre Company*. Undated. https://spidtheatre.com/.

Stone, Simon. *Yerma*. London: Oberon Books, 2017.

Tomlinson, Roger. "What Are We Counting?" *Arts Professional* (Magazine), May 25, 2017. www.artsprofessional.co.uk/magazine/article/what-are-we-counting.

Trust for London. "Islington." February 15, 2019. www.trustforlondon.org.uk/data/boroughs/islington-poverty-and-inequality-indicators/.

"UK House Prices 'Least Affordable Ever'." *The Financial Times*, March 17, 2017. www.ft.com/content/ea8f28fc-0b08-11e7-ac5a-903b21361b43.

Vaghaun, Meghan. "Jubilee." *Synonyms for Churlish* (blog), *Medium.com*, March 13, 2018. https://synonymsforchurlish.com/jubilee-chris-goode-royal-exchange-38d52b192108.

Wesker, Arnold. *Roots*. London: Bloomsbury Modern Drama, 2018. http://dramaonline.com. DOI: 10.5040/9781472525581.00000009.

1   Typical girls; or, the privately owned punk squat

Fran and Leni **by Sadie Hasler**
Old Trunk Theatre Company
King's Head Theatre, 115 Upper St, London N1 1QN
1 August 2017

By my lights, the best charity shop in London is the Cancer Research in Islington, near Angel Station. A certain kind of charity shopping requires a local population willing to throw away expensive things. I've found Maison Martin Margiela jackets discarded for one reason or another by their owners; Visvim, once, although it didn't fit. I flatter myself that I'm keeping to the thrifting tradition of fashionable art students, even though my own tastes are considerably closer to Miss Piggy's: "if it's expensive, it fits." In their London incarnations, charity shops offer the chance to dress a couple of economic orders above one's own station. You want to shop somewhere like Upper Street: a place that, as Tim Butler notes, has "been lifted out of the local economy into the global one," stocked with donations from those existing outside of the normal value scales of the nation.[1]

There is in a sense only one story these days about most of London's neighbourhoods: how expensive they are to live in now, relative to whatever point in the past, whether the 1970s, the 1990s, or five years ago. Regarding Islington, Charles Dickens Jr.' *Dickens' Dictionary of London* (1879) notes that "Houses here are very cheap."[2] The subject of considerable wartime damage, Islington has risen from the ashes to become a much-researched gentrification case. The sociologist Ruth Gass coined the term in 1959 to describe neighbourhoods like this one:

> many of the working class quarters of London have been invaded by the middle classes—upper and lower. Shabby, modest mews and cottages—two rooms up and two down—have been taken over, when their leases have expired, and have become elegant, expensive residences. Larger Victorian houses, downgraded in an earlier or recent period—which were used as lodging houses or were otherwise in multiple occupation—have been upgraded once again.[3]

As Lees et al. note, "Pioneer gentrifiers began moving into [the area] in the late 1950s."[4] The process was intensified in the 1960s by increased access to mortgages, in the 1970s by government funding for house improvements, and post-1980s by a wave of "Super-gentrification, or financialization," in which

> a further level of gentrification . . . is superimposed on an already gentrified neighborhood, one that involves a higher financial or economic investment in the neighborhood than previous waves of gentrification and requires a qualitatively different level of economic resource.[5]

The major controversy may simply be whether "gentrification," with its connotations of inherited English social forms, can adequately address property values driven upwards by these realisations of international finance.[6] What we who flow through the area have gained in the sort of people who are willing to throw out a £1,500 cotton jacket, we've lost in, well, what happens when those people enter a rental market. My friend, the corporate lawyer, kept occupied by 90-hour weeks, talks of being well past buying here—"it's what Chelsea was in the nineties," I'm informed. This is to say, suddenly unaffordable for the merely affluent.

Angel Station is still in TFL Zone 1. Islington is now practically central London, although this was not always the case: like most of the map of London, it began life as an independent village. Slightly uphill from the City, many of its locations are associated with water—indeed water sources in the area used to service much of the rest of the city. Sadler's Wells, now a dance venue, was named for the springs found on the property. Clerkenwell, named for Clark's Well, passed in and out of being fashionable. Justice Shallow allegedly brags about getting laid nearby.[7] In George Gissing's *The Nether World* (1889), the nearby Clerkenwell slums hosted the lowest levels of the Victorian poor. Gissing's actress heroine is disfigured in an acid attack—a form of attack back in the news in the summer of 2017, one taking place not far away at Highbury Corner. This latter attack bespeaks the area's continued proximity of extremes of poverty and wealth.

Pub theatres are a surviving Victorian form, an entertainment of the very poor. So-called *penny gaffs*, named for their low entrance fees and lower-class entertainments, were often just rooms in the backs of pubs, where broad comedy, agreeably patriotic violence, and even simplified versions of Shakespeare were performed. The King's Head's current iteration, as a pub theatre, is an invention of the 1970s. Dan Crawford, a visiting American, had the idea to open a performance space in a déclassé area. As Adam Spreadbury-Maher, the theatre's current artistic director, notes, 1970's Islington offered "hardly any restaurants. The roads off Upper Street were populated by musicians and artists because the rent was so cheap."[8] It was possible to do theatre in a tiny room to tiny audiences. Many famous careers intersected with the place: Tom Stoppard, Jennifer Saunders, Richard E. Grant, and Alan Rickman.[9]

The 1970s were also a different time for Islington. London as a whole still had a superflux of unoccupied housing. Squatting was, in parts of the city, a viable option—indeed one seeking to establish itself as a route to permanent settlement made possible by radically different laws about property ownership.[10] The *Squatters Handbook*, a by-product of this era, recommends the appearance of domesticity to prospective squatters. It is, for example, "a good idea to have some furniture with you when you occupy a house. It helps to show the police and the nieghbours [*sic*] that you are squatters and not burglars or vandals."[11] Squatters are advised to "always tidy up after you have entered," and, if possible, to improve the property squatted in. At least as the *Squatters Manual* describes it, it was possible to imagine squatters as essentially respectable neighbourhood members.

Considered 40 years on, punk and squatting—far from synonymous, although often overlapping—can be seen as part of the negotiation of who gets to live where in London. White squatters faced none of the racial barriers to housing market entry experienced by the Windrush generation of Caribbean immigrants. The cover of the 1978 edition of the *Squatters Handbook* foregrounds a well-scrubbed white child while her extended family tends to a Victorian arch. It's easy to be cynical about this kind of image, which, after all, was trying to make squatters seem as agreeable to the English mainstream as possible, down to its reliance on traditional gender roles (men reconstruct masonry, and women paint and rear). Their hair might be a bit longer than yours, the image suggests, but the neighbourhood was nevertheless gaining by its squatters some decent dinner parties—the sort of place where haloumi might have been served 30 years before you could get it at Nando's. It's not coincidental that by the 1970s England's councils were building less and less housing. This handbook announced an attempt to play nice within a city whose housing shape was more or less going to stay the same for a while. Home possession has a complex relationship to self-representation in the area—one that has continued even as property prices have become some logarithmic parody of what a middle-class economy can scale to.

Punk, the music and the attached lifestyle, attempted to give the finger to all of this bourgeois nicety—if without any particular structural commitments to political change.[12] Yet its concerns were the ying to the handbook's yang: what to do with disused space; what sort of non-traditional household to live in; how, broadly speaking, to fit into society. To burlesque "God Save the Queen," as the Sex Pistols did, was to keep the established set of figureheads in place: to at least agree to the same playing-field as those you were trying to piss off. Rather than imagine a different future, punk's most commercial face denied one: "there's no future," rather than a better one, "for you."[13] Several punk subcultures genuinely attempted to make better societies—and still do, to this day. This is not the story of punk, however, with which we're most familiar. Instead, punk's most superficial elements—teased hair and agitated guitars—quickly became its calling card.

I'm on my way to the King's Head, an Islington pub theatre, to see *Fran and Leni*. I would love to report that some of the best nights of my life have been spent at a pub theatre—like the man behind me at another show the previous week, declaiming loudly to his friend that the best thing he'd seen last year had been at the Hen and Chickens. These recent years of pub theatre programming, however, have left me agnostic. My theatregoing friends believe that overall the best years of London's pub theatres are for the most part in the past. On the one hand, pub theatres do grant as much awkward immediacy as anyone not actually a sociopath can reasonably be expected to handle. Some venues carve out particular niches: the Finborough Theatre in Kensington, for example, is consistently one of the highest-quality theatres in London, with a particular focus on reviving older plays. On the other hand, there's a wide variety of these venues, and quality control varies enormously. The seats are never comfortable. The actors are close enough that you wonder about their lives: what brought them to (say) a pub theatre on an overcast evening in August, while many of London's actors had decamped to Edinburgh.

There has been a King's Head Tavern in the present location on Upper Street, since 1543; one lost his, in other words, since the institution was founded. The current building, like frankly most of London, is Victorian—and charming, to boot. Brexit be damned, there's a developed wine list (A Spanish Valdemoreda, "Soft Stone Fruit-Floral") and a £16.50 Cheese & Charcuterie Board "served with toasted campaillou."

London is a city where social boundaries are rigorously enforced. And yet, three florid, well-heeled Islingtonites sit down at the table with me, without asking, and within moments are loudly ignoring me. Their faces suggest confidence, security, and, by the time the performance starts, alcohol. Something in their confidence has overridden the alleged English horror of invading someone else's space. The pub portion of the King's Head self-fashions with an analogous confidence: Alan Rickman on the wall, Rioja on the wine list, and John Lewis clothing on the clientele.

The theatre, in contrast, seems frail—frailer than I would realise, in fact. Before the performance, an employee reads us a five-minute riot act: they receive no money from the pub—indeed they have to pay a licencing fee; change in a bucket would be appreciated. I admire entirely the young theatre manager who gives this speech. She is calm and self-assured and wise in a way I would not be for another decade after her age. She tells us fiercely that the King's Head is the only pub theatre in London to pay Equity—that is, the agreed-upon union rate for their services—to those who work for them.

Good for the King's Head. There will always be people willing, for a few years, to make a go of a life in the theatre, before circumstances push them out. A certain amount of risk might even be encouraged among 21-year-olds. Equity, however, is what sustains *careers*. Anyone who goes to the theatre regularly is, if they're being honest with themselves, a big aghast at how solidly mainstream theatres skew towards youth. It can sometimes feel, frankly, like theatre provides a respectable stream of young bodies for the well-heeled to ogle. Those bodies bear it for as long as their class status lets them hold out; and then they're replaced by new bodies. There's only a short period of time to make a career of it, and reduced art subsidies mean that period is getting shorter.

Fran and Leni was performed by Old Trunk, a two-woman theatre company that receives Arts Council funding.[14] Sadie Hasler and Sarah Mayhew, the two performers, collaborate on the company alongside roles as film and television performers, columnists, and, in Hasler's case, as a working playwright. Their shows tour the country, appearing, for example, at the Manchester and Edinburgh Fringe festivals, and when in London at venues like the King's Head.

Charity shops, urban gentrification, space, class, and aging all come together in the play. *Fran and Leni* channels an older, more rebellious London, while remaining strenuously committed to the present-day values of conservative, property-owning England. *Fran and Leni* is a two-woman show that tells the story of a punk band, The Rips, active around 1980. They are, by their own admission, not terribly successful. They break up over Leni's unreciprocated crush for Leni, and then meet again decades later. They manage to avoid the most commercially exploitative elements of punk: as they explain, they were "Introduced . . . to Malcolm McLaren who barely looked at us."[15] Instead, they have a good innings amidst people who, we might say, were truly punk rock: "We got pissed with The Damned, nicked Joe Strummer's gum, and stood down the front at the Roxy and watched Ari Up, drenched in beer." Leni in time becomes a music journalist; Fran marries and has children. They finally meet again 20 years on, in 1996, when they reconcile.

We open at Foyle's Bookstore in Soho, being introduced to "music journalist, former frontwoman of legendary punk band The Rips, and author of *Ripped Tights, Dirty Knees*—Leni Delaney." These Rips have already passed into polite intelligibility, like Soho itself their wilder past days now largely contained in books. Leni's going to read, she says, and then "we're all going to get twatted." She's comfortable enough to drop vulgarities at a book launch. The play will tell us the story of her becoming the sort of person who is confident enough to do so.

It's the sort of people who write the memoirs afterwards that leave the best record of a historical era. A utopian space might have given us more rebellious punks—might have spent more time with their music, or with the frame-shaking vulgarity of what their bodies might do. *Fran and Leni* took the harder task of showing us young bodies aging—of reminding us of the consequences of living outside of mainstream life, its protections, and compensations. The production made its two characters up to be different ages. Leni seems to be in her early twenties, about the time we imagine her to be in the band. Even when dressed as a female punk, Fran's makeup made her up to be much older, perhaps in her early forties. This choice meant that the performance never settled comfortably into one timeframe, instead, like the script itself, constantly moving back and forth in time.

The action takes place on a single set: a grubby room in "The Pit," part of the squat where Leni lived. The walls show damp. There's an ironic picture of Queen Elizabeth. Making us focus on (say) the grotty spaces within which punk lives were lived is one of the best things that pub theatre can do: lock you into a particular space, making you focus on it, in a way that more sophisticated stage effects might obscure. These characters are never comfortable—and as audience members on uncomfortable benches, you're in there with them.

And yet the uncomfortable world into which we audience members were wrenched was also privately owned. The Pit, significantly, is not a squat. Leni finds a place to live through Pidge, a male acquaintance who never appears onstage. She describes it as a "Hostel for lost souls I guess you'd call it. Taking in waifs and strays makes Pidge feel better about being property-owning bourgeoisie scum." Forty years on, Pidge might have been the "property-owning bourgeoisie scum" (as I imagined them) that invaded my table. This slow alignment of imagined theatrical spaces and property ownership reflects what I term *resonant ownership:* the way that the space the stage represents is made privately owned rather than publicly contested.

Fran and Leni shows how difficult it is to imagine something like squatting from the vantage point of 2017. In 2008, the *Daily Mail* quoted the fabulously named Tory MP Eric Pickles, who had attacked councils who published the latest edition of the *Squatters Handbook*. Pickles wrote that

> [h]omeowners will be horrified that town halls are giving squatters the green light to break into law-abiding citizens' homes. . . . Promoting such lawlessness is breathtaking, but is sadly an indictment of social breakdown that has become rife under Labour and the prevalence of "human rights" laws.[16]

Yet *Fran and Leni's* small bias towards privately owned spaces sustains the Pickles imaginary. Fran and Leni may be rebellious, but in retrospect they were not living contrary to the housing laws. The culture moves forward, the culture moves back: we gain a new sensitivity to women's stories and narratives of queer lives, but lose the possibility of imagining life outside of privately owned spaces.

Graphics projected on the back of the stage reset the scene to "Creighton Comp, Muswell Hill, 1976"—again, while leaving all of the elements of the Pit in place, superimposing the past on them. Muswell Hill is a North London suburb, its relative lack of proximity to an Underground station giving it a somewhat out-of-the-way vibe. Originally built for middle-class Edwardians fleeing the centre of London, the ebbs and flows of urban demography had given the neighbourhood strong working-class associations by the 1970s—when a contrary ebb saw more middle-class families moving to the area, attracted to the then-cheap housing. What defines this neighbourhood is its so-called row houses, few of which are free-standing. The King's Head itself is not a detached building. The neighbourhood typifies the city's compressed privacy, each family's private world pressed together. From these houses, as from The Pit, you could have heard what the neighbours were doing; they, in turn, could have heard you. Indeed as a pub theatre audience, we spend the evening as close to the actors as their neighbours would have—in effect one row house over across the fourth wall of the stage.

Fran and Leni's relationship is created by the possibilities for class interchange created by gentrification. However, it also rewrites punk as a struggle for recognition within the private domestic sphere. Punk's ability to shock was always premised on its physical proximity to the normal and respectable. Like squatters, punks took over urban spaces, pushing to renegotiate what was important but not seeking to tear anything down. This shock outside of the household's walls mirrors what the play describes as an already-brewing crisis within it. Fran describes the middle-class family that pressured her to learn music as riven by internal pressures and crises. A typical incident involved her mother: "I caught her in the larder, emptying fucking jars on the floor. Custard powder everywhere." Within London's precisely defined world of houses and the descriptive words for them, "larder" pegs Fran's family precisely. Acquiring a larder—a room offering a separate space for food—is one of the reasons why a family might move to Muswell Hill in the 1970s. This separation of body functions—eating, sleeping, shitting, fucking—is what private houses have always offered. Yet Fran also describes these boundaries collapsing during her mother's breakdown. The slippage of "fucking jars" shows vulgarity, and even sex, encroaching on the custard, as domestic privacy goes off the rails for Fran's family.

Fran and Leni meet in the music room at their comprehensive school: a state-provided non-selective institution. In the 1970s, these comprehensives offered opportunities for students from different experience backgrounds to meet. Or as Leni, reading from her book, describes it:

Leni: So Fran was a proper musician. One of those kids who had been waddled along by her parents to sit on a stool like she had a rod up her arse at the age of five. I never had any of that. No tutoring, no love, but no rods up my arse either. I suppose I was a bit of a punk before I even knew what punk was. And Fran . . . was a nice girl. But not a prick.

Leni respects what Fran's family have been able to offer her: the "tutoring" and "love" that come along with a certain sort of "waddling." Significantly, this is the voice of the adult Leni, the writer: one who can appreciate the advantages provided by the waddling of class. As the play re-creates their first meeting, we see that Leni was not always so reverent of these things—as when they discuss *The Lion, the Witch, and the Wardrobe*, which Fran has read and Leni has not:

Leni: . . . Sounds shit.
Fran: It's a classic.
Leni: Exactly.

What transpires in the Pit is what Creighton Comprehensive began: make Leni into an educated person, capable of writing the book that both characters read from throughout the piece. When she first takes Fran, who has run away from her middle-class home, to the place where she is living, Leni calls it "Narnia"—revealing that she has read Lewis' book, supplementing the gaps in her own experience with what Fran has recommended to her. Even the no-place of the squat is retroactively colonised by the wardrobe, and the path to classed experience that it provokes.

What "punk" means to these women is an unstable thing. In part it is rebellion. There are fine shouted monologues for both characters, showing that the root of their anger is

Leni: All men. **Teachers** who peer down your blouse, **builders** who hound you from on high in the street, **a load of fake uncles** copping a feel the moment they can. All the moments of feeling trapped. Wolfed like a chicken leg. **All of a sudden I was in a rage and nothing could calm me down. It was the guitar** (*Fran: piano*). **Something in the repetition of the chords, the thrash and thrum, the pain in my fingers. It took me over from the inside. How dare they? HOW FUCKING DARE THEY? That's why we took to punk. Because punk took us out of all of it.** You think men touch girls like us when we look like us? You think they dare lay a finger. **Punk makes you see it all so clearly.** The filth. The squats. The piss in the alleys and no hot water to wash. But it's better than all the dishonest filth, the great big truth that hides; that **we are owned. We are property. We are meat.**

Fran, whose voice overlaps with Leni's in the boldface sections, has had issues with "Teachers" and "builders" and "fake uncles"; but Leni, speaking throughout, reveals that their invasions have progressed further on her differently classed body, hounded and peered at and groped. Both women are equivalently angry—"How dare they?" they say in unison, "HOW FUCKING DARE THEY?" Their alternating speech shows the different experiences they had of punk, defined by their different class positions. Yet even if middle-class Fran has not experienced the "piss in the alleys" with the same immediacy as Leni, she comes to the same conclusion: "we are owned. We are property. We are meat."

It is to try to escape these categories that the characters rename themselves. Francesca Jane becomes Fran, and Eleanor Rose becomes

Leni: Leni.
Fran: Like a man?
Leni: No, like a shitting Eleanor who hates her shitting name.

Their transformation into a punk group means changing the names they have been assigned, taking on names that may (as Fran suggests) transgress their assigned social roles. However, Fran and Leni's original names remain in the background. A former Eleanor is different from someone who had no posh name to begin with. The Rips—and her friendship with Fran—secure for Leni what her comprehensive school merely promised, her rise to the white-collar profession of writer. This is what Fran finally, in the play's present day, confirms for her:

Fran: It's really good, Len. Your book. It's honest.
Leni: You always made me feel like I was illiterate.
Fran: I know. That was wrong. You're not. You're a writer.

Fran confirms this by spending much of the play reading along with Leni, from her book, both actors speaking simultaneously. Fran, the older of the two, gave Leni the confidence to speak in the first instance. Leni's book reciprocally lets Fran express the ways her time in the band had exposed her to exploitation.

They jointly perform their recollection of being in the Rips as a time of pain and bravado. Leni describes her class origins as offering no straightforward way into becoming a musician. Instead, she takes one of the forms of initiative available to teenagers in her position:

Leni: That night, that guitar changed my life. I'm not exactly proud of the fact the first guitar I owned was nicked, but I'm not unproud either. . . . I sucked off the original owner after a gig at the Roxy a few months later and comforted myself we were square. You know, in the accounts department of my own head. Which is where it counts.

Forty years on, squalid blowjobs are as much a part of the collective memory of punk as the hairspray the two actors put as they "transform into punk" in front of us. But from the vantage point of 2020, we have a restored sense of the routine sexual exploitation of the young and unprotected involved in seemingly any mass cultural movement of the era. Onstage, the transformation involved the donning of dog collars and the application of hairspray, to the general wry amusement of audience and actors alike. This punk costume is not uncommon in London, particularly in the most touristed parts; you will occasionally see some committed teenagers on the Underground, serenely standing out. But punk is now practically as nostalgic as Edwardian dress—or, at the very least, about as dangerous. Zeibura Kathua, a former Londoner now living in Prague, describes how the "vaguely tribalistic net of interlocking subcultures" that defined London from the 1970s to the 1990s have now mostly disappeared in all but the most superficial forms.[17] With punk's presence as a threatening street tribe receded, the play reconsiders how unequally threat and danger were distributed among this tribe's members—noting that women received an inordinate share.

Reading from Leni's book, Fran and Leni describe the struggle to become something unlike themselves:

You think they'd do it to us, to girls who've grown their own fucking spikes out of their necks, like prairie cactuses? These collars don't say you can lead us like dogs, they say we will take your fucking arm off if you get too close. They say ask first, play nice.

They need to access language alien to Muswell Hill—"prairie cactuses"—to articulate what their adornments mean. Yet even as she describes this rebellious self-making, Leni seems to understand that she is simply choosing another form of fitting in.

These forms of hedonism, however damaging, led to the institutions dominated by the middle class: universities, bookstores, and radio reviewers. Leni's pornographic bravado chains her to the same institutions—the family, men—that she's trying to stand out from. When we hear her on the radio, we hear her at her most shocking, and most superficial:

Interviewer: What would you say to your critics?
Leni: I'd probably say something like, "Your dad came on my tits before he kissed you goodnight." Something like that.

The difference between this play and a radio broadcast, however, is the presence of the actors' bodies onstage, their mixed ages suggesting the wear of longitudinal exposure to a damaging cultural scene. In the last scene, alone with Fran, Leni reveals that her own father in fact used to abuse her: "Dad threw my DMs out after I accidentally kicked him in the head while he was—(*Mock cheerily.*) dragging me up the stairs." The provocative scenario she narrates—a bit of consequence-free fun for dad—is in fact a reclassifying, a reworking of the trauma; and it reverberates throughout everything else said cheerily about exploitation and violence. If *Fran and Leni* had been simply a radio program, it might merely have hinted at how incompatible living as a provocative radio voice can be with actual life. As a disembodied voice, as a punk persona, we can live like this: free from our past, free from consequences. But live performance reminds us of the liveness of bodies, the way that they can store trauma that a persona can cheerily ignore. The Rips' punk personas are simple, pat: surface vulgarians, living without regrets in a world of pleasure. Or, at least, of male pleasure—nowhere in their radio interviews do they describe enjoying themselves. Female pleasure is something obtained in private: "Sometimes you find yourself fury-fucking yourself in the bath and you don't even know why you're angry. . . . Did women masturbate in cave days? I hope we did. It sounds fucking dark back then."

Fran and Leni speak the words of Fran's book to reflect on their time in the media spotlight as horrifying. Punk traded them being noticed for participation in a media machine that finally benefited the men who ran the shows more than the acts they brought on. Looking out at their BBC audience, they were horrified to see

All those little girls in baby-blue jeans and happy T-shirts and long hair and shiny lips like wet cunts in the audience, with those old pervs' arms clawing their waists for the whole fucking country to see, old enough to be their dads, dirty old blokes who get away with everything.

During a projected video montage that accompanies this shared monologue, the set designer projected an image of Jimmy Savile, the BBC presenter only outed as a serial sexual predator after his death. These audience girls have not grown their own spikes. Yet Fran and Leni, too, have been exploited in ways their monologues suggest they have not fully appreciated.

Indeed this dismissive description of their audience, their lips after all "wet" to see The Rips perform, points to these women's discomfort with their own desires. The centrepiece of the play's action is a kiss between Leni, who wants it, and Fran, who is uncertain:

> For a moment **Fran** responds. It is almost something, then she pulls away, uncomfortable. She turns to the wall and wipes her mouth.

The wetness of Leni's mouth is unbearable to her; it needs to be wiped away. She turns to the wall—away from the wall the audience is seeing through, and towards a blank one that forms the boundary with another row house. She turns away, in other words, from desire that can be communicated, and towards being alone with her own discomfort; from something more open to something wholly private. This ends their relationship, the band—everything.

The two women go their separate ways. By 1986, when the last Police album was delayed by Stewart Copeland's polo injury, the bloom had gone off London's punk and postpunk scene—or, we might say, it had gentrified. London, not unrelatedly, was becoming the city we know now. As they recount their experiences of what happened next, both women's dialogue reaches into registers that seem vaguer and less thought-out than the hedonistic punk rock patter that they provide in interviews. Leni, again reading from her book, narrates finally finding a relationship:

Leni: . . . Then a girl called Tess wouldn't take no for an answer. Ha. She really dug the band thing. And she was an addict for pussy. What can you do? **Kissing girls is so soft. It's like you're undoing the years of men.** Finger a girl is like probing your own possibility, and when she cums, it's like being born. Fingers so far inside her it's like trying to track your own conception, **make peace with all the old stars as they shoot to land somewhere new, new universe, bright plants spinning.** Her cunt is a constellation and you're lost in space. And then, I tell you. You do not need a cock. You do not need a cock.

Both of the characters here try to articulate something they do not fully understand. Fran's reading along with Leni's words shows she is intrigued by the moments where Leni reflects on her sexual experiences with women—those that, by rejecting Leni, she herself rejected. Leni, meanwhile, speaks in the easy universality of cliché: one moment crude, the next idealistic. Sex with women gives a frame for describing what *she* wants, rather than what is wanted by the world of men. Leni has developed what she accused Fran of possessing: a "lofty middle-class musical ambition and barely disguised sense of entitlement," along with a stable partner and a household. Yet her history with this subsequent partner is also a retreat into Leni's individual experiences, which do not appear onstage.

When the women meet again, following Leni's reading, they confess what actually happened around the band's breakup. Leni describes being raped by their manager, as well as her reasons for covering this up:

Leni: I didn't want you to know he was just another dirty horrible little man. I didn't want you to feel dirty. You're so . . . undirty. Ripped my tights, the fuck. If I could lay out the rips that have been made by men they'd stretch to the moon and back. I've worn them like a choice. Punk. Ha. Cheaper than buying new tights.

    . . . Sweary messy girls who dare to walk around with their arse out in fishnets don't get the chivalry of the law. . . .

"Chivalry" stands out from the rest of Leni's dialogue—even in this sentence, it jars with "arse."[18] It feels like a word from a dialect she uses less frequently. Indeed the phrase "chivalry of the law" is more abstract, less precise, and more archaic than most of what she says. She's speaking fluently and vividly—but in a language that's still, after all of these years, slightly unfamiliar to her. Exclaimed on a stage set overseen by Queen Elizabeth, "chivalry" expresses Leni's desire for older forms of politeness, recognition, and protection—ideas for which she can find no vernacular, no present-day equivalent.

And Fran has gotten sick, withdrawing into her own household. Her description of terminal breast cancer, oddly but intriguingly, focuses on a small act of consumer choice and in effect an act of curation of the private domestic sphere:

No. I actually have actual breast cancer. I'm in chemo, Len. . . . Hence the scarf. Which is also shit. Fifty p, Oxfam. But I couldn't bring myself to buy a nice one. In case I die. And my daughter thinks she'd better not throw it away because it cost fifteen pounds in Marks and Sparks. So I got a shit one, like old ladies wear when it's raining. And I didn't even wash it. So that she'll know it's OK to throw it out. And I've stopped washing my hair because it hurts to see it come out quicker and, really, what's the point? So the scarf smells. It smells of greasy head and cancer. Because cancer smells, Len. It's gone beyond that stale charity shop smell of cheap washing powder and forgotten people and stale biscuits. I'm the bad smell now. So she won't keep it if I forget to throw it when I'm too distracted by dying and she won't be reminded of the brief time they thought I might be OK.

This is not to deny the chance for someone suffering from breast cancer an opportunity for self-representation. It is merely to note Fran's horror at being returned to the smells of the "forgotten people" who contribute, in this account, to the presence of walking into a charity shop. So solid is her imagination of her individual household, its smells and presences, that she cannot tolerate the notion of the traces of her diseased body remaining within it. Her act of choice is an act of remaining separate from these "forgotten," this grimy mass public, even after her death.

The play's women don't walk away from punk with what they had wanted. Fran does not even want her experience to be remembered by her daughter. She feels guilty for the middle-class life she has created, and even for the illness that might end that life: she is guilty "[f]or selling out, being married with a kid and a mortgage and a hatchback and . . . [a]nd a degree." Like Leni, she feels guilty for wanting what she wants—and for what she has gotten. The "dirty old blokes" got more from women's bodies than they could possibly have wanted; these women are ashamed of simply having these bodies. Jimmy Savile, OBE, would continue to commit crimes more or less in plain sight until his death in 2011. Those who made something of this era, like Leni, were survivors. But the space of this survival drew them into a private sphere with their families: outside of the law's chivalry, outside of the smell of the charity shops, and indeed outside of the stage representation that Leni's relationship finally exceeds. They become what could not be represented on this pub theatre stage.

Sometimes cultural analysis is too easy. Literally the day after I see this play, the King's Head announces that it will be moving: out of the pub, and into a custom-built space next door, as part of a new development called Islington Square. Mark Gatiss, another actor who found early success at the King's Head, says he is thrilled that the theatre is moving "upwards . . . and a bit to the left."[19] However indisputably true this leftward move will be in a literal sense, I wonder how it will work in figurative practice. You can't make this stuff up: overseen by the Sager Group of Saudi Arabia, Islington Square is described as "[a] new destination in the heart of vibrant Islington. Islington Square sits on the site of the former North London Royal Mail sorting and delivery centre. It will complement and extend the neighbourhood's existing and thriving community."[20] Condominiums start at £715,000 for a studio flat, approximately 26 times the average pre-tax annual salary of a resident of the UK.[21] The reader can play paint-by-numbers easy irony, if they wish: the former state institution converted into luxury condominiums; the rough-and-ready pub theatre, capillary in "the heart of vibrant Islington," transplanted into a yet-more-expensive part of global hyperspace.

"The future of the fringe is here," reads the press release.[22] For fringe *theatre*, this is almost certainly true, at least for London: the new King's Head's custom-built space, sustained by a combination of city sponsorship, mandated corporate contributions, and private donations, is one of the reasons why London's gentrifying neighbourhoods continue to have theatre spaces.[23] In fact, London's strong councils means it has been far more successful at this than many other cities. An Equity theatre, supporting sustainable careers in the industry, will remain in the heart of Islington—and, as we were reminded before this performance began, someone needs to pass the bucket. But to get into this new theatre, you will literally pass through a converted former post office into a privately owned space overseen by a Saudi real estate conglomerate. You will pass, in other words, from the Islington high street to this global anywhere—taking the public out of the pub theatre. *Fran and Leni* seemed to intuit this need and tendency to gentrify the past: understood where the theatre, and this city, seemed to be heading in this early August 2017.

I return to the theatre two weeks later, and now promotional siding for the development obtrudes into the street. Large LCD screens show a promotional video for the development. It's easy to binge on the easy ironies presented. The screens give a list of famous Islington residents, part of the neighbourhood's "heritage." These include, most prominently, George Orwell (50 Lawford Road, 27B Canonbury Square). For some reason they leave out V.I. Lenin (30 Holford Square and 16, Percy Circus), who I would have thought was at least as famous. The advertised interiors look like the stage sets of plays about the super-affluent—like those in *Consent* (2018), which I discuss in my conclusion. One of them has a *Home Design* magazine on its coffee table, like an Escher diagram of bland international interiors. The list of amenities include the expected: proximity to central London, great local restaurants, that sort of thing. The Screen on the Green, a long-standing local cinema, is featured. Rather perfectly, the film it's advertising is *I, Daniel Blake*, Ken Loach's 2016 film about a man falling through the cracks in the social welfare system. In *Riff Raff* (1981), Loach showed workers constructing new-built flats out of disused government buildings—in that case, a hospital, rather than a post office. Someone in the promotional office was either in a hurry to get a photo—or, plausibly, knew exactly what they were doing.

My wealthiest friends in London, like the corporate lawyer, favour neighbourhoods with this kind of "character": butchers, cheesemongers, theatres, that sort of thing. My friends in the global elite have to work, so they're too busy to use them regularly. But it's nice to have them there. I don't think my friends are badly intentioned towards the sort of people who traditionally lived in these neighbourhoods; indeed, those who managed to buy 40 years ago are still around. But in the London imagination right now there seems no alternative to property ownership; and this ownership is now priced to an international level. My friends generally like life in these neighbourhoods without the community bonds—or the tax obligations—that sustained local institutions. These neighbourhoods are a lifestyle to be dipped into occasionally, and this is indeed the convenience that the Islington Square screens promise.

Fran and Leni realise they're being paid to entertain teenagers at the behest of older, wealthier men. The King's Head will be another cultural resource—another mark of authenticity—kept alive by developers. I'm happy that this will be the case—the theatre's Equity commitment is no small thing. I wish it well, genuinely. Nevertheless, and for all that I liked the play, I hope that it will not be the only version of its time period that we remain familiar with. I hope the squats—or maybe just the stories of those who didn't buy their way out of them—will stay a part of the story.

Notes

1 Tim Butler, "Living in the Bubble: Gentrification and Its 'Others' in North London," *Urban Studies* 40, no. 12 (2003): 2476.
2 Charles Jr. Dickens, *Dickens' Dictionary of London* (London: Charles Dickens and Evans, 1879).
3 Qtd. in Loretta Lees, Tom Slater, and Elvin K. Wyly, *Gentrification* (London: Routledge, 2008), 4.
4 Ibid., 13.
5 Ibid., 130.
6 The landed gentry classes were, of course, always supported by international flows of money, hidden to one extent or another by decorum and prejudice. The Antiguan slave plantations that supported Jane Austen's *Mansfield Park* (1814) are the best-known fictional instantiations of the web of international capital flows that Regency society both envied and hid.
7 "This same starved justice hath done nothing but prate to me of the wildness of his youth, and the feats he hath done about Turnbull Street," William Shakespeare, *Henry IV, Part 2* (Oxford: Oxford University Press, 2012), 3.2.280.
8 James Morris, " 'It Moved Boundaries': 47 Years of King's Head Theatre Pub in Upper Street," *Islington Gazette*, August 7, 2017, www.islingtongazette.co.uk/news/herit age/it-moved-boundaries-47-years-of-king-s-head-theatre-pub-in-upper-street-1-5135943.
9 "About: King's Head Theatre," *King's Head Theatre*, 2018, www.kingsheadtheatre. com/about.
10 Squatting has a long and complex history in England, owing to origins in common law, its long-standing involvement with the process of land consolidation known as Enclosure, and associations with particular notions of common ownership. A piecemeal but thorough series of legal changes from the 1990s to the 2010s have made squatting effectively illegal. Moreover, the conditions that led to squatting in the 1960s and 1970s, particularly ownership claims that had been allowed to go unacknowledged, are practically unimaginable within London and its environs: even if unoccupied, property values means that London land rights are now intensely guarded.
11 *Squatters Handbook* (London: Advisory Service for Squatters, 1974), 6, https://archive. org/details/SquattersHandbook/mode/1up.
12 See, for example, the account of punk's initial depoliticisation given in Jon Savage, *England's Dreaming: Anarchy, Sex Pistols, Punk Rock, and Beyond* (New York: St. Martin's Press, 1992), 8. Roger Sabin defines the somewhat "amorphous" term to mean "a subculture . . . part youth rebellion, part artistic statement" that "had its high point from 1976 to 1979, and . . . its primary manifestation in music. . . . Philosophically, it had no 'set agenda' like the hippy movement that preceded it, but nevertheless stood for identifiable attitudes, among them: an emphasis on negationism (rather than nihilism); a consciousness of class-based politics (with a stress on 'workingclass credibility'); and a belief in spontaneity and 'doing it yourself.'" "Introduction," in *Punk Rock, So What? The Cultural Legacy of Punk*, ed. Roger Sabin (London: Routledge, 1999), 1–2.
13 "Lyrics to 'God Save the Queen' by the Sex Pistols," *Songfacts.com*, 2018, www.song facts.com/detail.php?lyrics=1621.
14 All details taken from "Old Trunk Theatre Company," *Old Trunk Theatre Company*, 2020, https://oldtrunktheatre.wordpress.com/.

15 Sadie Hasler, *Fran & Leni* (London: Methuen, 2016), unpaginated depository ebook. All in-text citations are to this edition.

16 www.squatter.org.uk, August 10, 2017.

17 Zeibura S. Kathau, "The London I Knew, Which I'm Not Sure Still Exists," *Medium. com* (blog), February 26, 2018, https://medium.com/@zeiburaskathau/the-london-i-knew-which-im-not-sure-still-exists-e092671e671.

18 Leblanc indeed uses "chivalry" to describe her mixed feelings at being accepted enough in a "tribe" of punks to begin to receive the exaggeratedly patriarchal protection of its male members (Lauraine Leblanc, *Pretty in Punk: Girls' Gender Resistance in a Boys' Subculture* [New Brunswick: Rutgers University Press, 1999], 21–24, 104).

19 Qtd. "The Future of the King's Head Theatre," *King's Head Theatre*, 2019, www.king sheadtheatre.com/news-blog/the-future-of-the-kings-head-theatre.

20 "Discover Islington Square," *Islington Square*, 2020, https://islingtonsquare.com/.

21 Zlata Rodionova, "Islington Square Development with Property Prices from £715,000 Aims to Become the Next Covent Garden," *The Independent*, February 2, 2016, www. independent.co.uk/news/business/news/islington-square-development-with-property-prices-from-715000-aims-to-become-the-next-covent-garden-a6848726.html.

22 "About the King's Head Theatre."

23 "Future of the King's Head Theatre."

Works cited

"About: King's Head Theatre." *King's Head Theatre*. 2018. www.kingsheadtheatre.com/about.

Butler, Tim. "Living in the Bubble: Gentrification and Its 'Others' in North London." *Urban Studies* 40, no. 12 (2003): 2469–86.

Dickens, Charles Jr. *Dickens' Dictionary of London*. London: Charles Dickens and Evans, 1879.

"Discover Islington Square." *Islington Square*. 2020. https://islingtonsquare.com/.

"The Future of the King's Head Theatre." *King's Head Theatre*. 2019. www.kingsheadthe atre.com/news-blog/the-future-of-the-kings-head-theatre.

Hasler, Sadie. *Fran & Leni*. London: Methuen, 2016. British Library Legal Deposit Epub.

Kathau, Zeibura S. "The London I Knew, Which I'm Not Sure Still Exists." *Medium. com* (blog), February 26, 2018. https://medium.com/@zeiburaskathau/the-london-i-knew-which-im-not-sure-still-exists-e092671e671.

Leblanc, Lauraine. *Pretty in Punk: Girls' Gender Resistance in a Boys' Subculture*. New Brunswick: Rutgers University Press, 1999, 21–4, 104.

Lees, Loretta, Tom Slater, and Elvin K. Wyly. *Gentrification*. London: Routledge, 2008.

"Lyrics to 'God Save the Queen' by the Sex Pistols." *Songfacts.com*. 2018. www.songfacts.com/detail.php?lyrics=1621.

Morris, James. "'It Moved Boundaries': 47 Years of King's Head Theatre Pub in Upper Street." *Islington Gazette*, August 7, 2017. www.islingtongazette.co.uk/news/heritage/it-moved-boundaries-47-years-of-king-s-head-theatre-pub-in-upper-street-1-5135943.

"Old Trunk Theatre Company." *Old Trunk Theatre Company*. 2020. https://oldtrunktheatre.wordpress.com/.

Rodionova, Zlata. "Islington Square Development with Property Prices from £715,000 Aims to Become the Next Covent Garden." *The Independent* (London), February 2, 2016. www.independent.co.uk/news/business/news/islington-square-development-with-property-prices-from-715000-aims-to-become-the-next-covent-garden-a6848726.html.

Sabin, Roger. "Introduction." In *Punk Rock, So What? The Cultural Legacy of Punk*, edited by Roger Sabin, 1–13. London: Routledge, 1999.

Savage, Jon. *England's Dreaming: Anarchy, Sex Pistols, Punk Rock, and Beyond*. New York: St. Martin's Press, 1992.

Shakespeare, William. *Henry IV, Part 2*. Oxford: Oxford University Press, 2012. Oxford Scholarly Editions Online. www.oxfordscholarlyeditions.com/

Squatters Handbook. London: Advisory Service for Squatters, 1974. Archive.org. https://archive.org/details/SquattersHandbook/mode/1up.

2 Brexit's dispossessed

My Country: A Work in Progress **by Carol Ann Duffy and Rufus Norris**
National Theatre/Warwick Arts Centre, CV4 7AL
25 May 2017

Boudica **by Tristan Bernays**
Shakespeare's Globe, SE1 9DT
12 September 2017

This chapter reflects on property's role in the resurgence of regressive mythologies in English theatre culture: the way that Brexit suddenly had playwrights reaching back to consider very old forms, which often changed or overwrote the actual history of England's varied, hybrid national culture, evoking regressive ideologies even at progressive venues.

Archaic concepts have a way of infiltrating your life here. I knew I had to move to London the day someone in a pub in Leamington Spa told me he was tired of "invaders" coming into his town. Leamington is a prosperous city in the Midlands, all of an hour and a quarter from London by train; there are parts of Greater London that take longer to commute in from. It's a bedroom community for Coventry and Birmingham, with many professionals working at the head offices of Jaguar and Land Rover. These, too, may have been the invaders he meant: they had jacked up house prices, making the city difficult to afford in a way it had not been even ten years before. But he was talking to me, and I'm not English. About a month later, someone walked up to me in the street and noted, my voice and accent unheard, that I wasn't from there. I wouldn't in any sense want to compare my experiences with those who had genuinely experienced harassment: I'm a white dude from Canada, the sort of Commonwealth immigrant even hardcore racists might see as one of the good ones. Nevertheless, a few months later I had fled to London, where I mostly get outed as a foreigner by older people at classical music intervals.

At that point, in 2015, Brexit seemed basically a punchline: something the Conservative Party had proposed as a sop to the crazies. Business wasn't behind it, and the country was in favour of business; that was the end of that. One indifferently argued campaign later, and all of a sudden the country was preparing to jump over a cliff. In one of the oddest political wrinkles of life in this country, I voted in the Brexit referendum as a Commonwealth citizen. This is *not* going to last, I wearily predict. Some newspapers are going to point out that FOREIGNERS CAN VOTE—overrepresented and over here—and that'll be that. Like the vast majority of people in Islington, where I then lived, I had voted Remain, then woke up to the horror of the results. I had, it seemed, misjudged the reality I was living in. The UK would only enjoy a few months as what seemed like the stupidest developed nation in the world; worse things were afoot in America. But at the time the pooch seemed well and truly screwed. Generation Easyjet, as the signs at Gatwick address us, had gotten our wings clipped.

I had fled to the right place. All of the city's boroughs voted at about 60% to Remain. Of course, I am one of the "citizen[s] of nowhere" Theresa May, the Prime Minister, would disparage at the next Tory party conference.[1] *My Country: A Work in Progress* was the National Theatre's attempt to sort of poke a head out of the London bubble and see what, exactly, had happened. It's credited to Rufus Norris, the National's Artistic Director, and Carol Ann Duffy, who at the time was Britain's Poet Laureate.

I love the National Theatre with a passion I feel for few things in this world. I think the height of civilisation is seeing a bad play there: watching a thoughtful, inquisitive set of professionals throw something at the wall and see if it sticks. I bask in the presence of full-on, glorious, subsidised art. And I truly admire how well the NT manages the near-impossible position of being all things to all people. The laziest arts columnist in this country can rouse themselves from a prosecco hangover and bang out 1,000 words on how the National is failing at its mission, understood variously as: representing the cultural interests of every single person in the country, of every single person in the country save foreigners, of developing new work, of keeping an old repertory in production, of doing more Shakespeare, of doing less Shakespeare, of not doing things that are confrontational enough, of doing Sarah Kane, of doing more plays about the football, of putting Jude Law in more things, of doing more plays with older actors—you take my point.

Southwark, where the National Theatre sits, was a separate borough—with separate laws—as recently as 1855. However, it has since passed into being essentially central London, even housing the Greater London Authority's City Hall. Since the Second World War Southwark has been a centre for the construction of social housing, if now at a somewhat slowed rate. Indeed, the reconstructed Shakespeare's Globe, when first proposed, was controversial for blocking proposed social housing. More recent development has been very different: the hyperspace alien ziggurat of the Shard, for example, with its mix of expensive office space, expensive hotels, expensive private residences, and expensive restaurants. In these very recent architectural developments, you can trace the shift in the country's focus, away from its own citizens and towards the needs of an increasingly wealthy global elite.

Of course, that money (some of it, if you're reading the *New Statesman*; not nearly enough, in the *Guardian*; far too much, in the *Times*) sloshes into the arts, too. One of the things I didn't understand before I moved to England was the extent to which art is subsidised to move throughout the country—a commitment extending from smaller companies like Old Trunk (see chapter 1) to the NT itself. Unlike in the United States, where for the most part new plays are written in New York and (less frequently) Chicago or Los Angeles, this country's arts organisations genuinely want theatre to speak to and move through venues across the country as a whole. *My Country* was created in association with an impressive lot of these: the Citizens Theatre (Glasgow), the Curve (Leicester), the Derry Playhouse (Derry/Londonderry), the Live Theatre (Newcastle), the National Theatre Wales, the Sage Gateshead (Gateshead), the Salisbury Playhouse (Salisbury), and the Strike A Light Festival (Gloucester). Even in London, it toured—to the Theatre Royal Stratford East, "a people's theatre" about four stops on the Jubilee Line from the actual National Theatre.

So, London's stages often extend virtually around the country—and indeed around the world. Simulcasting has made this more immediate, but what happens on an influential London stage also often reverberates in bodies around the world as these productions are re-mounted. For example, I saw *My Country: A Work in Progress* at the Warwick Arts Centre, at my university's campus on the outskirts of Coventry, about an hour from London by train.

Prior to the production, the NT had sent interviewers throughout the country to gauge the thinking behind their vote. *Verbatim theatre* involves staging quotes from material gathered from real participants. In practice, its veracity is a strange thing: as with an editor in a television booth, the compiler of one of these pieces has an enormous amount of power over what gets selected. This play presents voices that did not quite understand what they had said when they voted for Brexit, or what they were saying now. This irresolution was the best possible representation of the national mood: of a country betwixt and between, unable to sort out precisely what it was.

Voices from London were not solicited. Rufus Norris, the Artistic Director of the NT and one of *My Country's* co-writers, explains this decision:

> It was very clear that part of the rancour, the protest, was about the dominance of metropolitan, London-based voices telling us this is how we do things. . . . We thought the thing to do was to get out and listen. As a National Theatre, if we want this place to be a centre of debate at all, it felt appropriate to start with listening.[2]

My Country reached back to the nineteenth century in order to find an appropriate format for this sort of listening. One tendency in British politics of the last 30-odd years has been towards the devolution of powers to the various regions. Britannia, portrayed as a sensibly coiffed woman of middle years, calls characters representing six British regions into a national assembly: Caledonia, Cymru

(Wales), East Midlands, North East, Northern Ireland, and South West. They gripe for a while, then drink, then sing, then dance, and then relay how they voted in the Referendum. They are fractious among themselves; the country is not one big happy family. Yet there is also no one centre for disaffect, save perhaps for the relatively more affluent south—and, indeed, for the EU.

This representative choice is a necessary kludge—something that, depending on your point of view, might be said about the country's regional boundaries as well. Devolution has settled unevenly on the kingdom's different regions. Scotland and Wales each have national assemblies with a set of particular powers; those inclined towards the nationalisms of either region balk at the term "region" at all. Equally, political will exists to further subdivide some of these regions. Cornish independence would, for example, divide the South West. The Midlands, East and West, have historically struggled to define themselves independently.[3] The decision to have one actor play each region made them seem roughly equivalent, hiding differences in size, economic status, and population. The decline of heavy industry, in its way as much a character in this piece as anyone onstage, hit the regions differently: the industrial North and Midlands were hit hardest, while the more service-oriented economies of the south prospered through inherited advantages of wealth and greater access to world markets. At the same time, this staging asserted, all of the regions thought of themselves as significant, each a part of the national dialogue. I assume Norris' team at the NT knew that all of this was going to come across as a bit flat-footed, and did it anyway.

A woman walks onto the stage and immediately addresses us: "Nice one."[4] We're being congratulated for doing something unusual: turning up to a meeting, and one that was clearly at least somewhat optional. The times do not suit this sort of meting, it seems—we are to be thanked for doing something like a civic duty, for taking time away from freezer pizza and Netflix. The woman is sensibly dressed, of approximately middle years, and wearing the restrained power suitish of the contemporary female executive—no big 1980s shoulders, no overly inflected hair. For those so inclined, her blazer buttons evoke a faint naval heritage, but their brass has been downgraded to something less showy. She looks very tired.

There's something she can't quite put into words, but she'll try: "I just—I thought there should be listeners. Witnesses, if you like" (3) She speaks like someone not quite certain of what she's saying; she pauses, and tries again. Restates things, suggests that we in the audience should have a role in the proceedings ("if you like.") "I'll get this place sorted. And could you turn your mobiles off? Thanks." (3). "Sorted" is a particularly apt word for things: it's a word for a fix, performed quickly, but with the sense that the solution might be a bit superficial. She'll take care of the AV, if we can manage our cell phones. She's asking us to focus, for a bit, and listen—to not distract ourselves with things that are "mobile," whether our phones or (frankly) our identities. In the manner of a town hall meeting, we're going to be stuck with some people we'd normally never talk to for a while.

The play's theme and setting harken back to the nineteenth century, which we might imagine as a time of greater national consensus. Yet the Victorian forms appear around a slightly faded national sense of self. The woman removes a Britannia hat from her bag and tries it on. She's obviously a bit uncomfortable, but she's going to make a success of it, grimly donning the symbol of authority. It towers over her; she puts it back on the desk. The country seems uncomfortable being itself in a ceremonial capacity anymore. This is why Britannia thanked us at the beginning: we're going a bit above and beyond assembling together, she makes clear. As the stage directions note, "*The regions arrive promptly. During their arrivals Britannia is busily focused on setting up the room for the meeting*" (3).

The first to arrive is Scotland, frankly the most attractive character. He wears the nicest suit—with a tie, even. He's buoyant and bouncy, while Britannia is a bit edgy and fagged. He has movie-star hair and a cool accent. Everyone else is in cardigan and tie, or the female equivalent, save Wales in a voluminous jumper. Everyone calls Scotland "Caledonia," which is very posh indeed—like a mid-range sparkling water. He calls Britannia "Poor wee Britney!," and the other regions follow suit; he says he's agreed to come "For the moment, Britney . . . for the moment" (3). In manner and outfit, Caledonia is well put together; the other regions, slightly less so. Scotland of all of the regions came closest to leaving the UK in a 2014 referendum; his suit evoked other meetings elsewhere at which he would be the national centre.

The meeting has been adjourned to listen to voice from the country around the event of the Brexit vote: the 2016 national referendum on leaving the European Union. "[T]he last time we met," the South-West notes, "The Bay City Rollers were at Number One. . . . Seventy per cent of the UK voted to join the Common Market. 'By bye, baby, don't say goodbye. 1975" (4). A Scottish band named for a post-industrial American town, albeit one chosen at random from a map, the Rollers point towards one of the issues underlying everything: the end of an industrial narrative of progress that might tie the country together—the sort of thing that might create the national will (and the tax base) to build city halls or other civic institutions. It's significant that none of the characters are dressed in clothing appropriate to work in heavy industry. Instead, the regions appear in the sort of business dress as appropriate to air-conditioned Bangalore as to Peoria.

London's voices were represented purely by those of politicians from Westminster. However laudatory the idea behind this, in practice this was beyond dystopian. Otherwise, the city was silent. This book as a whole tracks the reasons why the production did this, even stressing the urgency of stepping outside of the London bubble. But I found this representative choice completely oppressive: like having a baboon sit on your chest as in a nightmare, choking off your attempts to say anything. "But what about the Australian baristas here on one of those bonkers short-term visas only Australians get?," I wanted to shout; "what about the Canadian university lecturers who can vote?" I assume a lot of Londoners wanted to shout similar things. But of course the story of theatre is mostly that of people suppressing their freedom to talk, in order that the performance can continue. And so I sat, like thousands before me, and listened to the voices unfold. Norris explains what he wants the play's audiences to experience:

> I'd love them to experience some semblance of what the gatherers experienced. They came back saying how humbling it was that the more they spoke with people, the more they realised how judgmental they themselves were and how much they were living in their own bubbles.[5]

Everyone in the audience laughed whenever the regions introduced themselves in their native accent. I had a harder time telling apart their differences: it seems as though everyone not in the South fancies their region as the home of wan, lyrical, heavy-drinking cynics. The South, alone, is rich and smug: bringing organic food to the banquet, happy about the value of his house. The NT had chosen voices that typified the various regions; that was in a sense the purpose of the exercise. But this choice in personification also excluded the possibility of playing against type. It didn't seem totally unreasonable to be able to find something like Geordie Pizza in the organic Southwest. Similarly, if you fancied hummus (or even quinoa) in Leeds, you were playing against type.

Meanwhile, rootless cosmopolitan that I was, I squirmed. This seemed at times to be a play written by and for the British. I was also terrified at the vision of the country that was being presented: one where I, and many of my friends, didn't get to speak. "Does anyone, um, *foreign* live in the UK?" I asked the American friend I was sitting next to. (Which is a bit unfair: migrants were given stage time, if not in vast amounts.) *My Country* spoke loudly to the economic migrant's primary fears: that at heart the country's support for you is heavily contingent; that at any moment it can shift. Your rights are never permanent; they are special arrangements, subject to change at a seeming whim. Most of the time our lives are in the grey in-between of these special circumstances: you are allowed (up to a point), you are given rights (but not in full.) Voices throughout *My Country* were calling for something else entirely: a return to black and white, us and them, in or out. Was this what London felt like to the sort of people you see quoted in news articles, scared of the different accents and references to things they didn't understand? Did they, too, not see their own voices represented whenever they visited the city?

This was, after all, an opportunity to listen—I was part of the sacrament as well. Town Halls are a particularly Victorian institution: multiple-purpose rooms intended to encourage assembly, discussion, and debate, built during a time of greater investment in public services. They're potentially endlessly open to metaphorical readings: expansive and cold, drafty and overheated, falling down in places that have seen cuts and beautifully refurbished (or in danger of going condo) in the posh bits. When Britannia comes on at the beginning, it even took a minute to get the A/V working—an example of the necessary awkwardness involved in being a space used by multiple groups of people. Town Halls in our present era of austerity are always going to be a little bit grimy, a little bit falling apart, a little bit behind (say) a corporate conference facility. Indeed these days, if they are in good repair, it's usually because they're rented out at a profit. And yet they still function, particularly at moments of unusual community crisis or coming together. In London we vote in them; we meet with the transport authority or local councils at open houses or citizen forums; community groups, often representing particular national groups, rent them out. The greater density of English cities, and the proximity so many of them have to Victorian building, means more of the population lives near them than to equivalent structures in, say, the post-war American suburbs. Even if they are the sort of place you have visited only once or twice in your life, for some slightly awkward community function, they do resonate with the daily life of much of the population.

All of the regions had shown up in business dress—something that was never questioned, nor particularly acknowledged. Britannia's crown, symbol of some national status existing beyond merely going to work every morning, was the only thing that would look out of a place in an office. This detail reflects much of what is dreariest—and, in a sense, saddest—about the national discourse at the moment. Rhetorically, every aspect of this country's advertised life is frantically, obsessively pro-business—"Business Is Great Britain," as one ongoing government campaign puts it.[6] Ads for primary school teachers on the London Underground stress their role in creating future entrepreneurs. Whether for Leave or Remain, for reasons articulable or otherwise, all of these people—these regions—possessed no distinguishing characteristics in terms of dress, save this business focus. Work seems to be, as even the title alludes to, in progress—indeed there is no escape from it. The regions swear, drink, and dance in business semi-formal, but they never remove it.

And so, everyone has arrived. ("Promptly," the stage directions note, hewing to national stereotype.) Down to business. The script calls its first section—six long, unedited verbatim speeches, performed by one of the actors representing each region—the "six arias." As that term is used in opera, it refers to a long piece by one singer. Arias are often the showpiece numbers of a given opera—and here, too, they set the tone for what follows. The most resonant of these—the one I will confess I find myself thinking of, months on from the play—comes from Scotland, but really could come from most places in the UK:

> **Caledonia** *(William)* When I used to go to school, we'd look at . . . Fettes over the road with its massive sweepin driveway . . . and the castle that we used to call Castle Duckula. . . . You know frae the show? . . . An right from the start and eve—huh, even ore so when they explained tae me that my school was actually owned by their school. That ma school, the council just rented it from them. And that they also rent the Police Headquarters land and right the way up to where Telford College used to be. That's all owned by Fettes School. And you can't buy any land on that land. You can only lease it for ninety-nine years and then it reverts back to Castle Duckula on the hill.

And yet the fees for that school were some of the highest in the UK. And you see them aw troopin out in their nice academic uniforms wearing Harris Tweed jackets, ken what I mean? And they walk past aw—ay—us scheemies. And they got different times tae come out of school so they would never interact with us and the boarding school thur. . . . They would come out and they would literally buy two big bags of sweeties and their stuff ken to get them through the week or whatever. Now I'm no sayin that these kids were any happier or any . . . b—You know . . . I'm just sayin that they are set up. They ar taught that money just brings opportunities and that value of life. Whereas our school over the road were always kinda just sorta subconsciously told . . . they're the masters.

(11–12)

Fettes School in Edinburgh, attended by among others the former Prime Minister Tony Blair, is exactly what you might imagine an extremely expensive private school—the sort of place whose alumni are called Old Fettesians. William's verbatim speech reflects on what some of those opportunities are: to recognise who is symbolically in control of their community, from sweeties to sustained land ownership. They have, as "Castle Duckula" suggests, the quality of vampires: undying, feasting off the land and its people—even infecting the way their children see Saturday morning cartoons, now unimaginable without the lurking presence of economic circumstance.

This land ownership issue, in particular, seems particularly bizarre to anyone not from the UK. The vast majority of land purchases here are not outright: even when you buy property, your estate usually does not own it in perpetuity, what would be called a freehold. Much property in the country is in fact what is called a leasehold, which reverts back to its original owner at the end of a fixed period of time, often (as William notes) 99 years. As William describes, even the council—the city itself—has to pay homage, and indeed money, to what is already one of the wealthiest institutions in the area. And when many of these respondents hear "EU" they think of another layer of ownership—another triangle in the pyramid stretching above them.

The mood of these arias is in general uncertain. Other speakers reflect on changes that have occurred among different walks of life. Barbara, voiced by the North-East, notes that

when we started we were shepherding on ponies. So now it's motorbike and the dog . . . dog skills definitely dropped. People don't even have dogs now on some farms which I find incredible. The whole thing is geared up to big business.

(12)

Barbara and William share a dislike of the "big": the forces that truly shape their lives, as they see them, whether the established social hierarchy or the more naked fact of the business money that had longed propped it up.

In contrast to William and Barbara, who describe themselves as the lower classes within a hierarchical country, we have Jane from the South-West. I did not warm to her. Clearly an older lady of means, Jane frankly knows how good she's had it:

> **South-West** (*Jane*) . . . Twenty happy years in Bristol. . . . We are, the baby boom's generation you know, we are the, you know I was born in 1947 . . . you know, so yes, you know, we have lived this life where we've seen many, many changes. . . . OK I'm a lucky lady, look at me, I'm middle class you know and I've got a good good man, who has you know, made a beautiful home for us, you know, I'm very very conventional. We've always been you know been, I don't know if cocooned is the right word.
>
> (14)

Jane, a Leave voter, gives the laundry list of things her generation got lucky with: home ownership, freedom from foreigners—even conventional middle-class life itself. Despite being cocooned, Jane will nevertheless speak for others who are, she claims, "overwhelmed by immigrant labour." (Jane might well find my own presence as asphyxiating as I did hers.) In her final comments, she reveals her imperial ambitions: "I sometimes think this country could do with a benign dictator and I'm the one to do it!" (56). She is used to having her opinions respected—as, indeed, the Leave vote attests to. Jane's generation began in the cradle of the "cradle to grave" welfare state. They have consistently dismantled the former as they move towards the latter. More than a regional divide, Brexit also showed a sharp age distinction: the Leave decision was the old of the country voting to overrule the young.

The "sacrament of listening" is a clunky phrase, but *My Country* was serious about it. Having the same actor play all of the different parts from one region, regardless of background or gender, was also a profound gesture of sympathy. It allowed an actor to focus on regional accents with care—indeed no one appeared, so near as I could tell, as a stereotype, beyond their own will to self-stereotype. Implicit was that, given time and circumstance, we might all have wound up like any one of these people. We were witnessing voices to speak to one another who in daily life would certainly never have come into contact. They reminded us that in a time of shrinking opportunities, we are all in all likelihood stepping on someone else's toes, getting on someone else's nerves. The play dramatised this quite well: some of these people seemed really noxious—yet in another context, you could imagine their stories being quite sympathetic.

Jane's use of the word "overwhelmed" suggests the cultural force, the gnarled-up inchoate unease, lurking behind the economic rationale to leave. Keeping in this vein, the other regions consider themselves even worse off than Jane in the Southwest: "We have sent them billions. And when you see what has happened to Brussels it has all been completely redeveloped" (16). England's post-war redevelopment has been particularly uneven. The reasons for this are various and sundry, ranging from the world's investment in the Marshall Plan but not in redeveloping Britain, to the country's own lower tax brackets and unwillingness to invest in infrastructure. Countries such as Germany, France, and the Scandinavian countries held on to a greater extent to industrial bases; England's economy drifted towards service and the South. Whatever the reason, patches of the country are in bad shape, relative to life in its higher-tax European neighbours. London and the South, held aloft by the finance industries and their knock-on effects on the economy, have proven an exception to this. Indeed the news around Brexit, before and after, was full of the ironies of the vote: many regions that benefited heavily from EU development money voted heavily to leave. From the various voices, we hear a litany of complaints about the EU:

> The EU doesn't work. . . . The EU's wrecked the fishing industry. . . . [Y] ou've got the flow from the EU which comes from the UK and then the rules which the UK Government make which then impact on Scotland. . . . [W]e weren't in the European Union whe-when the war was on and things like this and we were self-sufficient then.

(16)

Indeed, "[m]emories of World War Two are central to many Britons' self-image as an indomitable island people."[7] The ways in which the Second World War has been used to whip up patriotic frenzy in this country have done, and continue to do, lasting damage: with regard to Britain's relationship with Europe, but also in terms of the nation's relationship with itself (and indeed with reality). The virtues associated with the war—communal sacrifice, solidarity in the face of a common threat—have been held in cultural prominence but political abeyance since the 1980s. The thousand fractious involvements of the day-to-day life of a modern state, investigating rail service in the Northeast and testing grapes for pesticides in Inverness and making sure the airports meet their employment quotas, are so much more complicated. As much as the main character in *Yerma* (chapter 6), many of the respondents in *Our Country* longed for an end to uncertainty: "THIS IS MY COUNTRY," Donna from the East Midlands tells us, "And if I had to I'd fight for it" (31).

Talk among the regions swung to the traditional sources of British self-regard: orderliness, good government. Party on, Niamh from Northern Ireland: "I was in Barcelona and I was up on one of those Gaudi buildings and we were on the roof and we were walking on an undulating roof and there was not a hand-rail." Niamh vividly, if a trifle comically, attests to how nationalism can keep you from seeing the finest things in the world because of your focus on what is familiar. Handrails were hardly the main objection to Europe, of course. And from here we entered into the horrifying dark heart of Brexit. I won't over-cite this section; it's hard going, even on the page. But it mostly went this: "It's like murderers and rapists from other countries. Pisses me off. Pisses me off big time. We just had some of them Syrians coming here" (24). These were voices spoon-fed by the right-wing newspapers:

> If you live in Peterborough, Boston, all these small communities have been overwhelmed by immigrant labour. . . . You don't feel as safe in the city as you used to. . . . Seventy-five million now in Britain. . . . There are no Christian churches in Saudi Arabia, but when they come here, they're allowed mosques.
>
> (23–31)

Islamophobia was the rawest part of what these voices told us, but the pushback was more universal. The rights of Christians in Saudi Arabia became a pretext for kicking the Bulgarians out of Reading. There were, to be fair, some positive responses to foreigners. Bless you, Caledonian Glenn: "I'd open the doors to all of them, quite frankly" (25). Yet decency and acceptance seemed provisional, like things that could be turned on and off. Acceptance was grudging, hard-won, and reversible; intolerance could leap up like an electrical fire.

One of theatre's particular qualities is that it's hard to leave. You are, of course, free to head out at any time—but your presence is noted. You are a walkout, adding a frisson of interest—of scandal—even if you're just heading out to deal with some bad shellfish. But of course most of the time you just sit there, having ideas come at you, unable to do much with them. Theatre makes you focus—and focus we did, as grievance after grievance after grievance was aired. I saw anew the curse of having a long history: it provided an off-switch to thinking about specifics, a conciliatory set of ghosts to set around the table, and a minimally acceptable dog-whistle to anti-foreign sentiment.

And then, in the midst of it, we heard from London: from David Cameron himself, as yet unaware of his place in English history: "we have got, I think, the most successful multi-racial multi-ethnic democracy on Earth, it's a matter of huge pride to people in this country, huge pride to me" (25). At that moment my heart swelled. This was my side: I was after all a skilled economic migrant, over here to take a British job. It said so right on my visa: without this guaranteed job, my residence in the country would be literally impossible. I was momentarily on team Dave-O: summoned here for the work, strong believer in migration—and, yes, genuinely proud of British multiculturalism, much of which was created by the hitherto utterly mundane fact of economic migration. Watching this all dissolve back into nativism before my eyes was horrifying.

It all gathered to a head, griping, fighting, bellowing at enemies: Muslims, Germans, paedophiles, and Syrians. It was time for the country itself to intercede, breaking up the fight. "Britannia, my name is Britannia," she corrects the various characters onstage. And she delivers an oration: an attempt to remind the voices of something larger than them, something that pre-existed and survived us. It appealed to a shared experience:

> I am your memory, your dialects, your cathedrals,
> your mosques and markets, schools and pubs,

your woods, mountains, rivers . . .
your motorways and railway lines, your hospitals,
your cenotaphs with paper poppies fading in the rain.

Particular, precise, obsessed over the sort of public services we cling to, but are no longer willing to fund comprehensively: Britannia sounded like the present moment, and not inclusive. The railways work, but barely; the NHS survives, but in a state of normalised crisis. And, yes, all capped off with war nostalgia, mouldering in the rain.

All fine and well—and in its own way, moving. But before Britannia moved on to the results of the Brexit vote, she delivered an oration that seemed more symptomatic than diagnostic of the country's issues with the world:

I have breathed you in, like air,
and breathed you in as prayer, or speech, or song.
I am your heartbeat and I take your pulse.
Who else but me can praise your ancient, living
language as a jewel?

In its modern form English is not a particularly ancient language. Tamil, say, in a recognisable form is 2200 years old. A native English speaker of the present day requires heavy coaching to read Chaucer's English (ca. 600 years ago) and would find the English of a hundred years before that unreadable. It is the unusual global citizen who locates the heartbeat of the English language in, say, Hull. I felt myself coming over all Caliban: didst thou teach me language, Carol Ann Duffy, so that I could pass the naturalisation exam? At this great expansive moment, the voice excluded migrants, foreigners—indeed the vast majority of the English-speaking world. The island nation expanded to hear its own voices, but sunk deeper into itself.

I needed a drink; the regions needed a vote. But first, they gathered to share food. I have attended throughout this book to the ways that hedonism, usually sexual, marks in contemporary London theatre a tendency away from certain sorts of shared political commitment. Here, it was carbohydrates and alcohol that limned the death of political consensus. There were elements of the changing, slightly more multicultural nation incorporated: the East Midlands offer "Saag Paneer. Also Red Leicester" (40). The Northeast offered a Geordie Pizza: "It's a pizza base, yeah, with a topping of just chips" (40). Heavily invested in differentiating its regions, the country seems to have lost interest in distinguishing its starches. The talk instead returned to the pleasures of the body, at which North-eastern sensualists also excel: "At least if you come with us you'll get laid, Britney. We have the most sex" (43).

We returned to shagging and ill health. Many of the sacrifices asked from the nation during World War II were met with promises of what would happen afterwards. The country did not simply ask for austerity forever: this was a spirit of sacrifice entered into for a set period of time, and shrugged off as soon as it was feasible to do so. And yet the contemporary UK uses the slogans, and the aesthetic, of inter-war sacrifice to justify low government spending. But, of course, the UK of 2017 is not the UK of 1953. Nevertheless, it has been a rich country discursively ruling itself like a poor one: constant cutbacks, a seemingly endless faith in "business" and "entrepreneurship"—an overweening fretfulness, as though the country's way of life itself were under siege. And as those like Southeast Jane show, even material success and comfort do little to assuage this.

An elephant in the room was, in a sense, the room: London, from which this production sprang, and which was deliberately silenced by the creators. So, as the regions begin to chide each other for their social problems—obesity, drink, and child endangerment—London was always the point of negative comparison: "Regrettably, Newport in Wales has the highest rate of drug trafficking outside London" (42). This is what London connoted: crime, foreignness—illicit substances brought into the country by an outside force, however ardently they may be consumed domestically.

The vote is taken, region by region. Brexit happens. Sitting in my university's auditorium in the East Midlands (which voted Leave), it sunk in again:

> **North-East** (*Bill*) Last night I felt more British than I'd ever felt. We were in a damp shed, brewing tea, pouring down rain, freezing cold. Committed to a project that is far too complicated for wa [us]. That, to me, is Britishness.
>
> (55–6)

Where to locate this addiction to failure—to the sad and lame, the uncomfortable, the cold, the uncertain? Product of a different country, I felt a seam of something truly alien here, in the invocation of the dark and cold: alien, but familiar, from my time living here. Even rhetorically, my country, Canada, is not good with helplessness. We can't be—the weather would kill us, I guess, or at least push us back into our condominiums. To hear someone describe a political decision—an irrevocable choice—that was too complicated for them to understand made me shudder. Bill sounded like Lear: reason not the need! And we all know how Lear winds up. Bill's statement is funny, rueful, and self-defeating—but made in the name of huge numbers of other people. What if you hate damp, are indifferent to tea, and think of complexity as something to be embraced and managed? Is this still your country? Does it want me? I stumbled out of the theatre, onto a train, and back to London, thinking dark thoughts. My response to the deep unease with foreigners had pushed me back into myself—had made me clannish, in the face of so much clannishness. The piece spoke to a general stripping of the ways to imagine being a foreigner in England. There was no project to join, no unity to imagine, and I was no entrepreneur.

While I was writing this chapter, I went to see *Boudica*, by playwright Tristan Bernays, at Shakespeare's Globe in the Southbank. It was a long day: reading and writing about Brexit during the day, and then seeing what was clearly a post-Brexit play in the evening. It was a startling spectacle, not least because the

Roman procurator at the beginning of that play was wearing Britannia's crown from *My Country*, or thereabouts. I'll say this for Bernays and *Boudica:* they were playing with political fire, in the way that the best theatre should. But it certainly marked a further retreat into clannishness, here suggested as going back centuries.

Although now a part of the London firmament, the Globe, farther up the South-bank from the NT, has proven a resiliently controversial enterprise. The experiment itself is, of course, avowedly retro. From the beginning it has been dogged by questions of historical accuracy—although even what "accuracy" means is up for debate. No actual plan of the original Globe exists, and of course such a structure would not meet modern-day fire codes and other safety rules; the theatre is a compromise between what we can ascertain from historical plans and what legal rules permit. The style of performance is also a continual compromise. Recently, Emma Rice, the Globe's third artistic director, resigned after only a year in the position. Among other controversial moves, Rice installed a more extensive lighting and sound rig into the space, angering those who thought the space should remain closer to less adorned Renaissance-style performance.

The Globe has a uniquely difficult position, albeit one faced by a lot of other arts organisations. It does not receive extensive government subsidy, yet its Bankside location and iconic name give it a quasi-national status—and of course it also benefits from this iconicity. Yet it must straddle a probably irreconcilable set of it interests: of tourists and purists, of mutually unrecognisable kinds of nationalisms.

In any other time I might simply have found *Boudica* ridiculous. I mourned that earlier innocence, and the ability to properly scoff at fake Shakespearean dialogue ("I'd rather walk in blood than walk a slave / For he thy Emperor!"[8]) At times of political uncertainty, I guess, we reach for iambic pentameter. It gives us a framework into which to stick our jangly thoughts; it ensures that something will line up, even if the ideas don't. Yet Boudica was also, alarmingly, written from what was clearly a consolidating post-Brexit mindset. The Britons at the beginning of the play complain about Roman tax collection and bureaucracy—dog-whistle words for the anti-EU crowd. The Roman soldiers speak with London accents—but then commit a truly startling act of child rape, of Boudica's daughters Alonna and Blodwynn. This is in the sources, but nevertheless my jaw sagged—not only at the act itself, but also at what Michael Billington termed the "Brexit-baiting" of the evening in general.[9] The Roman aristocrats were effete, rapemongering diplomats who complained about the weather. The lazy conflation of sword-point Roman rule and that of the EU, which Britain had voluntarily entered into, made the play's politics an affective hodgepodge of violated honour and violent reprisal. The rabble-rousing anthem that began the second act was the Clash's 1979 "London Calling," sung as the British hordes prepared to march on London. At another moment, Andraste, Boudica's patron goddess, floated down from the rafters in a twentieth-century flight suit and helmet. All of British history—the druids, the Clash—floated in a chowder of anti-European sentiment.

Boudica's second act attempted to make the situation more complicated—but here again, a play's attempt at patriotic inclusivity neglected to mention anyone not technically born within the country. The Britons slaughter innumerable Roman civilians. We meet Silvia, a Roman settler woman, when Alonna saves her from an attack. "We were born here," Silvia explains, citing her own connection with the country. Anyone who simply moved here for work was written out of the narrative, save for the profiteering Roman administrator class. Further, all of this talk happened on a stage where far more interesting, violent things were happening. The Britons got fight scenes, music, an onstage goddess, and Gina McKee from *Notting Hill;* the Roman foreigners got to talk about their conflicted sense of belonging.

Of course, it all goes badly in the end. Boudica's revolt, as the sources say, is put down; her daughters are left wandering in the wilderness. It doesn't work, but it looked great while it was happening. I was reminded of North-East Bill, drinking tea in the rain: awed by the complexity, the theatrical pageantry, of something not entirely thought through. And the fight scenes are among the best I've ever seen staged; the rainy mid-September night was beautifully atmospheric, particularly with a seat indoors. The lighting was gorgeous. Stage smoke mingled with illuminated steam evaporating from the performers. They were having a good time, at *Boudica*—and even I was starting to, fully against my will. "You Britons, hear me! For Britons are we all": Boudica speaks to us, her people, towards the end of the play. Twenty years on—if this play is ever revived—I fear that this voice may speak to two sorts of people in the audience: to the native-born, and to tourists.

There was a time when that might have been me: good colonial a bit awed by the Globe, impressed with the myth of British distinctiveness. And indeed the world market for British distinctiveness has long propped up some disquieting sentiments in the UK itself. A certain kind of Canadian paleoconservative wanted Brexit to happen as ardently as any UKIPer, that the English-speaking peoples remain unsullied by EU lightbulbs. Indeed, viewed from overseas, the spectacle is better: Britain truly reminded the world that it existed through the Brexit process, if not in a particularly good way. I thought of Donna from the Midlands, announcing that she was willing to fight for her country, whatever her country was; I thought of "invaders." The fight scenes were slick and electrifying—among the best the UK stage could offer. There was none of the dutiful, self-consciously lame gathering of voices that appeared in *My Country:* no Geordie pizza, just bureaucrat blood. The play portends one sort of English future. I hope I don't have to live there.

Notes

1 Qtd. in Tom McCarthy, "Does Theresa May Really Know What Citizenship Means?" *The Guardian* (London), January 21, 2017, www.theguardian.com/books/2017/jan/21/theresa-may-citizenship-tom-mccarthy-aeschylus.
2 Qtd. in Amelia Gentleman, "Rufus Norris: 'We Are Living in an Age of Extreme Selfishness'," *The Guardian* (London), February 27, 2017, www.theguardian.com/stage/2017/feb/27/rufus-norris-we-are-living-in-an-age-of-extreme-selfishness.

3 See, for example, Ben Truslove, "Does the East Midlands Have Enough of a Regional Identity for Devolution?" *BBC*, November 4, 2014, www.bbc.co.uk/news/uk-england-29745031.

4 Carol Ann Duffy and Rufus Norris, *My Country: A Work in Progress* (London: Faber and Faber, 2017), 3. All subsequent citations are given parenthetically by the page number.

5 Qtd. in Gentleman, "Rufus Norris."

6 "Business Is Great Britain, UK Government: Department of Business, Innovation, and Skills," September 21, 2011, www.gov.uk/government/news/business-is-great-britain.

7 Estelle Shirbon, "Brexit Debate Brings Out Britain's World War Two Fixation," *Reuters UK Top News*, June 3, 2016, https://uk.reuters.com/article/uk-britain-eu-worldwartwo/brexit-debate-brings-out-britains-world-war-two-fixation-idUKKCN0YP1XO. A full discussion of this phenomenon, pre- and post-Brexit, exceeds the scope of this study, but see, for example, Lucy Noakes and Juliette Pattinson, "Introduction," in *British Cultural Memory and the Second World War*, ed. Lucy Noakes and Juliette Pattinson (London: Bloomsbury Methuen Drama).

8 "What's on: Boudica," *Shakespeare's Globe*, 2017, www.shakespearesglobe.com/theatre/whats-on/globe-theatre/boudica-2017.

9 Michael Billington, "Boudica Review—Gina McKee Reigns Supreme in Brexit-Baiting Epic," *The Guardian* (London), September 14, 2017, www.theguardian.com/stage/2017/sep/14/boudica-review-gina-mckee-brexit-shakespeares-globe-london.

Works cited

Billington, Michael. "Boudica Review—Gina Mckee Reigns Supreme in Brexit-Baiting Epic." *The Guardian* (London), September 14, 2017. www.theguardian.com/stage/2017/sep/14/boudica-review-gina-mckee-brexit-shakespeares-globe-london.

"Business Is Great Britain, UK Government: Department of Business, Innovation, and Skills." September 21, 2011. www.gov.uk/government/news/business-is-great-britain.

Duffy, Carol Ann, and Rufus Norris. *My Country: A Work in Progress*. London: Faber and Faber, 2017.

Gentleman, Amelia. "Rufus Norris: 'We Are Living in an Age of Extreme Selfishness'." *The Guardian* (London), February 27, 2017. www.theguardian.com/stage/2017/feb/27/rufus-norris-we-are-living-in-an-age-of-extreme-selfishness.

McCarthy, Tom. "Does Theresa May Really Know What Citizenship Means?" *The Guardian* (London), January 21, 2017. www.theguardian.com/books/2017/jan/21/theresa-may-citizenship-tom-mccarthy-aeschylus.

Noakes, Lucy, and Juliette Pattinson. "Introduction." In *British Cultural Memory and the Second World War*, edited by Lucy Noakes and Juliette Pattinson, 1–25. London: Bloomsbury.

Shirbon, Estelle. "Brexit Debate Brings Out Britain's World War Two Fixation." *Reuters UK Top News*, June 3, 2016. https://uk.reuters.com/article/uk-britain-eu-worldwartwo/brexit-debate-brings-out-britains-world-war-two-fixation-idUKKCN0YP1XO.

Truslove, Ben. "Does the East Midlands Have Enough of a Regional Identity for Devolution?" *BBC*, November 4, 2014. www.bbc.co.uk/news/uk-england-29745031.

"What's on: Boudica." *Shakespeare's Globe*. 2017. www.shakespearesglobe.com/theatre/whats-on/globe-theatre/boudica-2017.

3   Transnationalism

Rotterdam by John Brittain
Arts Theatre, Great Newport Street, London WC2H 7JB
24 June 2017

I was taken to *The Phantom of the Opera* on a school field trip when I was 11, and that was it: I've attended the theatre ever since. Anyway, I have *Phantom* on as I write this and it's hard not to wince, a little bit: those antique drum machines. Yet I've never seen a more important play. I assume John Brittain's *Rotterdam* (2015), performed at the Arts Theatre in Soho, is going to be *Phantom* for a lot of people: something they were taken to in school, something that pushed them that little bit into the modes of aesthetic engagement and sympathy for others that theatre promotes. It's worth reflecting on the uses to which blunt-but-effective drama can be put. Equally, however, *Rotterdam* gives evidence of an inward turn in the British mind, and an emphasis on privatisation, that Brexit only intensified. Throughout the chapter, I think particularly about what I term *buy-in:* the way that plays seeking to open progressive topics to wider audiences ground their stories in things that are widely palatable. The play illustrates the compromises necessary to translate the process of gender transitioning for a wide English audience in the present cultural moment: specifically, a turn away from European engagement.

Rotterdam was first staged at Theatre 503, a fringe venue specialising in new plays. That venue itself is a bit of a transplant, whose moves around the city trace theatre's continual need to find affordable spaces amidst gentrification. Starting as the experimental space above the Gate Theatre in Notting Hill, the theatre moved to a permanent space over the Latchmere Pub in Wandsworth, South London. London's contrasts are pretty evident in this area, subject to a hyper-gentrification more recent—but far more intense—than that experienced in Islington. As recently as 1971, the region was low-density enough that Covent Garden's wholesale fruit and vegetable market could be moved there. In these last 20 years, the sort of development typified by the Nine Elms development near Vauxhall Station has placed a forest of new high-rise buildings into what had previously been a mostly industrial and working-class area. A lot of theatres willing to develop new writers sit in the region, like the Ovalhouse atop Oval Station and the Battersea

Arts Centre inland from the new condominium rows of Vauxhall.[1] As we will see, in its 2015 first performance in rapidly gentrifying Wandsworth, amidst newly built condominiums and established social housing, *Rotterdam* reflected the story of the gentrifying classes: those with private means to take full advantage of state support.[2]

Plays that succeed in small, further-out venues often transfer to the West End—as did *Rotterdam*, after winning an Olivier Award for Outstanding Achievement in an Affiliate Theatre. The production was, then, subsidised and not subsidised at varying parts in its life cycle: the recipient of Arts Council funding in its original venue at Theatre503, but a commercial proposition by the time of its West End transfers. These transfers allowed it to engage a much wider audience. And yet the economics of renting a West End house mean that even the smallest of these venues cannot be as intimate, or as adaptable, as a small fringe space. In its first West End transfer in 2016, *Rotterdam* appeared in the downstairs space of the Trafalgar Studios, off Trafalgar square—one of the smallest West End venues. Donnacadh O'Brian, who directed that production, calls these West End spaces "unqueer": less malleable, less particular, than Theatre 503's more adaptable fringe space.[3]

The Arts Theatre, where I saw *Rotterdam* in 2017 in its second West End transfer, began life in the 1910s as a members-only club putting on plays that would be banned for public performance under pre-1968 theatre censorship. It was in the Arts Theatre in 1955 that Peter Hall first directed Samuel Beckett's *Waiting for Godot* (1953) in English. It may also well, by the time you're reading this, not exist, at least in its present form. Having been purchased by a private investor, the current development plan is for "The Arts Theatre . . . [to be] be demolished, with only the original building's façade and a Grade II listed 17th-century townhouse left standing. The complex will also include a 66-bedroom hotel with a rooftop swimming pool."[4] Although a theatre will be reconstructed within the space, the focus of the building will not be theatrical. The developer promises instead "the largest bar in Theatreland."[5] The seats in the space's new performance space will not be permanent, and the performance area will be much smaller.

Soho gentrified earlier and more comprehensively than has Wandsworth to date. Once a centre of gay and lesbian life in the city, Soho has been for many years a hyper-commercialised, hyper-expensive part of central London—its few remaining gay bars now largely either closed or expensive tourist attractions.[6] By the time something makes it to the expensive West End, its potential for leaving things unresolved or experimental is limited.

Rotterdam follows in the long tradition of the so-called Problem Play, one that addresses a contemporary social issue through a well-established plot playing out in an aspirational setting. These plays usually have a definite shelf life, tied to the issue that they address. *The Second Mrs. Tanqueray* (1893), Arthur Wing Pinero's play about a woman whose sexual life was rendered extra-marital owing by a technicality in international marriage laws, is a historical curio. But in its time *Mrs. Tanqueray*, which first appeared at the nearby St. James Theatre, was part of a discussion through which nineteenth-century society worked through new and complicated ideas. It's not that everyone in Britain in the 1890s thought that a woman who had Fallen needed to be shunned. But what appeared in West End Houses was not necessarily the most intellectually advanced thinking, but instead an attempt to use an established plot to think about new ideas. These blunt instruments knock ideas into the mainstream, buy-in heavy and, as a result, often innovation-light. Our social crises and their resultant problem plays are going to seem like curios in a hundred years—but this is not to diminish their contemporary importance. Problem plays are by their nature bellwethers, responsive to their audience's sense of what is normal in order to nudge it slightly in a new direction.

Much theatre attendance occurs out of cultural duty: the feeling that exposure to the theatre, as to sunlight, is salutary. This is what brought me to *Phantom*. The content of the play can be secondary to the experience. *Rotterdam* will do good work, rendering the issue of gender transitioning into something recognisable to a wide English demographic and giving trans audiences a resonant presence on the stage. So Yas Necati, writing in the *Independent*, writes that "*Rotterdam*'s narrative made me feel proud to be trans, and I identified with the loss as well as the determination of the main character."[7] In particular, Necati notes the way that this character was able to sort things out for themselves. In this way, the play tells an aspirational story of generational and gender self-determination. *Rotterdam* marks an important moment in normalizing trans experience on the West End stage. It achieved audience buy-in, however, by appealing to some of the contemporary nation's most traditional narratives about itself, particularly those associated with privatisation and the withdrawal from Europe.

You walk to the Arts Theatre, mostly likely, from Leicester Square Underground Station; other options include Tottenham Court Road and Oxford Circus. This half mile is maybe my least favourite in London: tourist central, with confused foreigners milling about in exactly the same confused, vaguely stoned way I do when I travel. Regardless of how well-grounded you are, Leicester Square at most hours of the day is a confusing experience, to be navigated as quickly as possible on the way to somewhere else. Something analogous is true for the characters as well. *Rotterdam* is about a late-twenties English lesbian couple, Fi and Alice, living in the Netherlands with Josh, Fi's brother. Alice has not yet come out to her parents; Fi has come to realise her gender dysphoria and begins transitioning male. Fi becomes Adrian as the couple briefly break up, Alice having a brief relationship with Lelani, a Dutch woman. Adrian and Alice reunite, and they decide to move back to England.

We open in a living room, fragmented into pieces. The actors are already on the stage when you arrive in your seats, miming their daily lives over loud Dutch pop music—at least, in that slightly stagy way that unmarked everyday real life gets communicated onstage. Most of the time, we're not engaging in gestures that communicate the essence of our personalities to people in the cheap seats, but of course this is exactly what an actor needs to do. Alice, clearly some sort of professional, pecks away worriedly at her laptop; she interrupts this occasionally to kiss Fiona, her girlfriend, dressed as the more conventionally butch of the two. Twentysomething club kid Lelani puts on her makeup, pouting in front of the mirror. Buy-in inveigles through legibility. Making all of these characters so readable flatters the audience: we're given time to get to know them, to suss out what they're going to become over the course of the play. Alice looks worried about something; Fran is clearly holding something back from Alice; Lelani, bless her, just wants to have a good time, as she applies makeup the colour of the set's lamps. Even here, we notice the differences between English and foreign characters that will define the play. Alice's fretting conveys a frustrated interior life. Lelani in contrast is all immediacy and exterior display.

Alice and Fiona's living room is the space into which Rotterdam intrudes, photographs of the city printed across their furniture. There is, indeed, one of Berkhoff's anticipated sofas, on which Alice sits. Fi is anxious because of her gender dysphoria; Alice is anxious because she has not come out to her parents. The elements of their life in the Netherlands appear as reality-interrupting devices distorting a realistic stage picture: Lelani a few feet away from them on the stage although geographically somewhere else in the city, Dutch pop music blaring over their routine conversations. In what follows, Fi and Alice will sort out all of these interruptions, not only integrating their sexualities into a cohesive multiple-generation family but also returning to England. As Una Chaudhuri writes, particularly of nineteenth-century realism,

> The fully iconic, single-set, middle-class living room of realism produce so closed and so *complete* a stage world that it supported the new and powerful fantasy of the stage not as a place to pretend in or to perform on but a place to *be*, a fully existential arena.[8]

Rotterdam's staging suggests a middle-class living room in potential, fragmented by these intrusive elements. A more experimental stage framing might have permitted a more challenging or progressive notion of wholeness than that of Fi and Alice moved back to England and reconciled with their families: might have embraced transnational experience, rather than showing it as an annoyance.

This fractured domestic space becoming whole shows class capture—the normalization of middle-class experience—working internationally. It makes its English characters a little older, wiser, and more directed than Lelani. Despite what a reviewer terms its "fun, fun, fun" façade, *Rotterdam* is at heart a play about a middle-class professional couple—a lawyer and a teacher—briefly engaging with a less rooted younger person, and then severing the connection.[9] Lelani's self-exposition as a gay woman who has come to Rotterdam inadvertently reveals her housing instability and lack of a definite career trajectory:

Lelani: . . . My parents were like, "You've finished university you need to come and work with us," and I was like, "No way, I'm going to go and live in the city." And they were like, "No, we don't want you to do that," and so I was like, "I don't care, fuck you," and then I came here on my own and called Wouter and he made me his assistant and let me come live with him.

Alice:	Right. Wait, hang on, you live with Wouter?
Lelani:	Yah. And his wife and kids. It's pretty awkward. But he doesn't charge me rent. 'Cause I think he's in love with me or something. But I am not interested. 'Cause he is really old. And I am gay.
Alice:	Oh. Right.

(15)

Lelani does not treat her sexuality as a particularly significant aspect of herself—not unimportant, but not even the most awkward element of her ménage with Wouter. She is what one reviewer terms a "gay-manic-pixie-dream-girl," less a fully rounded human with future plans and present needs than a shiny plot contrivance.[10]

Lelani's matter-of-factness about gender and sexuality exists primarily in contrast with Alice's more tortured take on the subject: "**Alice** . . . y'know, we all have that awkward stage when we go out with men, don't we? / **Lelani** No. I came out when I was ten" (45). In the problem play, complexity—encumbrance within the snags of the plot—gives people dignity and even full humanity. Lelani's nineteenth-century antecedent would be something like the female servant Christine in August Strindberg's *Miss Julie* (1888), able to take a lover without incurring the full mechanism of the tragic plot but also limited to serving the principal characters. In reinforcing stereotypes about complicated foreigners, the humour here does not contribute to any meaningful social change or awareness. It simply reinforces traditional ways of thinking.[11] Brittain, in a post-play discussion, describes Lelani a bit provincial: "She's never been away from a small village, a small town," where "she's always been the coolest person." Despite being a "really confident and out-there person," she displays a "naivety" even an "ignorance" towards the central characters' plight.[12] Lelani instead offers what foreigners traditionally offer Anglo-Americans in overseas coming-into-sensuality narratives: showing them how to live a little bit more before they return to their indigenous domestic tension. Foreigners live in the moment, but knitting together a lasting relationship of complex individuals is the province of English characters. England is far from the only country to fetishise the daily habits of those in other countries—in particular, their sexual habits—as breezy and uncomplicated. Nevertheless, the Brexit moment highlighted how readily the problem play's apportioning of simplicity and complexity matched how England (or, we might say, a dominant trend in its thinking) sees the rest of the world.

Resonant ownership in the play is limited to a laptop—but this is not to limit how significant this device is. Alice's computer was the most realistic element of the onstage props, undistorted by colourful lighting or exaggerated furniture. It did not open up magically to reveal Lelani billowing in smoke from a nightclub, like the dresser. It was perhaps the part of the staging most deeply resonant for its younger audience members. I am roughly the age of the play's characters, and I took exactly the same Apple notebook with me when I moved overseas. (All that is solid melts into your Macbook Air.) The laptop anchors Alice in the world—and in ours. Information drawn from the Internet is their central point of contact with trans culture. In failing to bring other people onstage to offer any perspective on this Internet solipsism, *Rotterdam* confirms rather than challenges the way our laptops can lock those working out of their countries of origin into a transient, disconnected mode of life. This mode of consumption-driven lifestyle colonialism could have happened anywhere in the world.

As with many other plays in the book, *Rotterdam* used interruptions in normal timing to consolidate rather than question the most prevalent stories the London bubble tells about itself. As the fragmented stage set implies, *Rotterdam's* actions occur during what is a liminal life stage for the two characters, as Alice and Fiona/Adrian sort out their lives around Fiona's gender transition and Alice's coming out to her parents. Within the play's mostly realistic staging, these lives are repeatedly pierced by a mild form of interrupted time, in a device borrowed from television situation comedies. The word "beat" appears frequently in the script, indicating both a pause in speech and a significant moment of mutual recognition between two characters. These beats in conversation show the unsaid at the edge of being articulated: a pause before a truth is revealed. However, these moments also show the slow dawning of the desire for home in the English characters:

Lelani: Come out with me tonight.
Alice: What?
Lelani: Come out with me. Tonight. In Rotterdam.
            Beat.
Alice: I . . . I can't.
            Beat.
            I have to go home. Sorry, I'd like to. Really.
Lelani: You are not just being polite?
Alice: No, I'm not just being polite.
Lelani: It's fine. There will be other times.
Alice: I don't know about that . . .
Lelani: Why not?
Alice: I don't think I'm going to be here much longer.

These sitcom-like pauses invited the audience into the characters' thinking, making their move from confusion to acceptance readable. Audience and characters alike move, via these pauses, towards feeling comfortable with the social and relationship shifts that occur around gender transitioning.

Despite Rotterdam being just across the sea from England, while living in it both Alice and Fiona stand apart from their English families and from Dutch society. This gives them a space, free from interference, to figure themselves out. Alice's private health insurance funds Fiona's transitioning without issues. Britain's National Health Service (NHS) would support gender transitioning, but it would take longer to get appointments, and would involve less individual freedom in choosing the locations of clinics.[13]

Indeed Alice and Fiona's privatised independence follows an ideological path that differs from those of both their conservative and liberal sets of parents. Alice's parents are conservative enough that she has never come out to them, despite her living with a female partner for many years. Fiona's parents, in contrast, are English lefties: "You never had this problem, your parents didn't care, they've done drugs, they go on protests, they think Jeremy Corbyn's too reactionary." Fiona relies on her parents' social inclusivity, but ignores their socialism. She describes a dense world of North London signposts: drugs, demos, Jezza when he was simply a backbench MP. North London's socialism, stalwart if patchy, remains typical of the place in a way that is no longer true of other regions of the country. Fiona's parents are fine with her gender transitioning; they would be less OK with private health insurance, at least as a general principle.

Rotterdam would be a different play if it had reflected on the social ethics of gender transitioning: how it should be funded and how a health care system should deal with it. The end of the first scene, for example, gives us a moment whose bring-the-curtain-down form would not be out of place in a nineteenth-century play:

Alice: It's alright, you can tell me—
Fiona: I know, Alice, please—
Alice: You can tell me—
Fiona: I think I'm a man. *Beat. It sinks in, then HE repeats.* I think I want to. . . .
            I think I'm meant to be a man.

The stage directions clarify something that we can only intuit in the production: that *this*, telling his girlfriend, is the moment when Adrian transitions. This is a moment of private self-determination rather than something worked out in society alongside other people: "I think I want" comes before "I think I'm meant," the individual's wish coming first.

Fiona moves forward quickly with transitioning. This is one of the first plays I've seen to really capture how the Internet now structures our daily lives. Whether learning to knit or changing our assigned gender, we start with a Google search. Fiona's brother Josh gets, as the play's characters note, slightly too into the online research:

Josh: Alright, some other day, or there's a place in Delft that have a drop-in
            clinic, and they're open some evenings—
Fiona: Great, that's great, just bookmark it.
Josh: Already done, and there's this forum on this website that has a list of all
            the online support groups you can join.

This moment of quick Internet search and instant, disembodied connection aligns Josh and Fiona with the audience. I had booked my ticket to see the play online, too—in fact this is how everyone in London, for the most part, does things now.

I read reviews, checked the venue for seating angles, and—even though I had been to Leicester Square a hundred times before—my cell phone lead me to the venue, whose location I can never quite remember. My manner of booking connected me to Fiona's gender transitioning, framed as the latter was like a consumer experience: something we research online and proceed to by the most direct route.

Fiona's coming out as transgender to her parents parallels the start of the Dutch new year. Writing in *Time Out*, Tim Bano sees this coming out as part of a generational narrative: "Congrats, millennials, I think we've made it," he writes, noting that this is one of the first depictions of this generation onstage.[14] However, Fiona's speech makes clear that she sees her decision as also reflecting her English family's inherited traditions:

> Mum, I think I'm transgender. *Beat.* Yeah, like, I'm a man, but born in a woman's body. Yeah, they're both here, I've told them. *Beat.* Thank you. I love you too. Yeah, I know, I know that. Yeah, yeah, I er . . . I want to start living as one, I think. No, I don't need any money for anything, I'm alright. I don't know. I don't really know what happens next. Yeah, she's alright, I think, you're alright, aren't you?

Alice: is not alright.

Fiona: No, I haven't told anyone else. You're all the first. Adrian. Yeah, after Granddad.

(40–1)

Fiona tells her family what is going to happen. By not being onstage, they do not get to control the encounter. On the other hand, granted this freedom, Fiona returns to family tradition—freely, and of her own volition.

This is at once expansive national sexual politics and regressive international class politics. The Netherlands provides a space for hyper-particularities, like the *bitterballen* Lelani feeds Alice in a club, or vast universals, like the search for identity. Nothing in between really appears. Alice and Fiona do not meet any other transgendered people within the play, save through the Internet. The couple's social circle is made up entirely of direct relations and one intimate partner. *Rotterdam* shows being middle class as knowing how to speak and act authoritatively. The "beat" device is premised on the notion that even your silences are perceptible, and that they matter to other people. Alice's accent marks her as slightly posher than Fiona, but Fiona's description of her family life suggests that her family is the inner-London ying to Alice's outer-suburbs yang. They are both slightly different variants of the city's representationally dominant classes, and they have taken the city's bubble with them overseas.

In contrast to Lelani's brusque, straightforward statements about her sexuality, Fiona's description of her reasoning is both opaque and private: "I dream as one. *Beat.* In my dreams. I'm a man. Every time" (23–4). Adrian offers no further description of his reasons for wanting to transition; he does not describe how he worked this out in terms of his everyday life. He does not seem to be the member of any sort of community dedicated to gender transitioning; the idea seems to have come in dreams, in private, rather than through any social experience. Stated in such terms, Adrian's wishes can chime with a wide range of audiences: even someone who has never known a trans person will presumably have had a desire for self-determination that has set them apart from their society.

Having given this account of self-determination in very general, and so potentially widely resonant, terms, the play also addresses the human need to know how the mechanics of sexual intercourse work for people who are different from them. Indeed, sex becomes the biggest stumbling block to Adrian and Alice's relationship as it appears onstage. Despite the fact that Alice seems shocked, there is something slightly clinical in the language she uses to describe her objections:

> It means I don't want to suck on the end of a dildo like it's your penis. OK? I don't want to touch it. I don't want it inside me. And I don't have to justify that, I just don't want to do it!

> (64)

The graphically sexual elements of their private lives are here again mediated by something they purchase. In this *Rotterdam* reflects a larger problem with plays about transgender experience. As described in a survey by the performance artist Sunny Drake, a

> number of trans artists commented that many non-trans creators fixate voyeuristically on certain trans experiences, such as the physical transition. With this, there is often a focus on the 'before-and-after' spectacle, details of our surgeries and hormone therapies, and the 'reveal' moment when the audience discovers someone is trans.[15]

As Drake writes, such accounts of trans experience neglect both the idiosyncrasies of individuals' decision to transition, and the wider communities that shape and sustain such transitions. "While hormones and surgeries are important to many trans people," Drake notes,

> they are not the sum total of our experiences. At a community level, trans artists are creating nuanced work about a whole array of topics including family, relationships, racism, substance use, colonialism, immigration, and technology. I do not see these priorities filtering through to professional theatre.[16]

Drake's description reflects *Rotterdam*, which keeps gender transitioning at a relatively straightforward level: dreams fulfilled, strap-ons contemplated. The characters do not encounter economic problems. Adrian is fortunate enough not to need to work: she quits her job ("It's a Christian school") after they do not allow her to discuss gender transitioning with her children, and the discussion of money drops from the play (62).

Some of this deck-clearing and community-limiting is necessary to attach gender transitioning to a conventional story. To critique *Rotterdam* as a sitcom ignores how widely messages encoded in that medium circulate, provoking awareness and discussion. Adrian must nevertheless experience an utterly conventional breakdown. Over pounding dance music, he staggers home drunk and tried on a series of his old dresses, finding that none of them fit. This is exactly what characters in movies do, shouting, weeping, and pounding away at a mirror. He even challenges Josh to a fight: "Don't push me, hit me! You think I'm a man? Come on then! Hit me! Hit me! HIT ME!" (84–5). In giving Adrian space to be so emotional, the play confirms that his transition is important; that self-determination matters enough to warrant this full commitment of the theatre apparatus. (There's a mirror scene in *Phantom*, too.) As Drake suggests, however, it also frames transitioning as a series of key moments happening to individuals, rather than as community stories told over sustained periods of time.

This is true for the play's international community as well. Lelani, finally, does not wind up as part of the family restored at the end of the play. She becomes in the end one of those foreigners existing to show buttoned-up Brits and Americans a good time. Her housing situation and blank acceptance of Wouter's advances is played as comedy. But she could also be the subject of a different play about young people, where her sexual dependence on an older man for housing and employment could lead to grimmer consequences. Instead Alice and Adrian reconcile in the final scene, holding hands as they wait in the ferry terminal for a boat back to Hull. And already this play's era, where British young people might regard time in Europe as a normal part of their development, seemed to be slipping slightly into the past.

Brexit happened between this play's first performance in 2015 and the restaging that I saw in 2017. This was not a young person's movement. Voters over 65 were about twice as likely as those under 25 to vote Leave.[17] Adrian and Alice would both have been able to hold their jobs through the guarantee that EU citizens can work anywhere in the European Union; I would not put them down as Brexit voters. Yet the Brexit decision revealed unthinking affinities between mostly progressive groups like theatre-makers and the more conservative parts of the electorate. Its broad emphasis on lives in transition leads *Rotterdam* to treat its foreign setting as liminal: pop music, pub snacks, and convenient lesbians, but no place to remain. Adrian's only interactions with non-English people are with the school that fires her and with the man in a bar she nearly picks a fight with; both interactions happen offstage. Throughout the Brexit campaign, those on the Leave side claimed national self-determination was paramount. Britain, they claimed, would do a better job figuring itself out at home than in the EU. This is what *Rotterdam's* main characters decide, as well.

To make it in the West End, it helps to be certain in what you are. Less focused as a pure theatrical space, the new Arts Theatre will lose some of its capacity to creative disruptive theatrical illusions. Analogously, *Rotterdam* limits how disruptive Adrian's transition is. It shows a confident gender transition—one that is available to affluent young people with private insurance, able to operate without the sort of community support and entanglement that might lead to a more complicated, less focused account of the process. It does not claim to be the only such story. All major cultural changes need this mode—a romantic comedy, or something similarly accessible—to become more widely accessible. I'm bullish on the play's shininess: *Phantom* did a lot of work for me, as I'm sure *Rotterdam* will do for others now in what was my position. Plays popularising progressive positions have a greater-than-average claim on inherited forms and traditional opinions.

Nevertheless—I'm sure what follows from here might be beginning to seem predictable. At various points in writing this, I've put in and taken out what seems like the easiest kinds of points-scoring: *of course* everyone in the play is white, and *of course* everyone speaks English. (Although they are, and they do.) My biggest concern is with *Rotterdam's* sense of the mainstream, and with its resulting lack of interest in connecting with the country in which it was set. It didn't need to have a sofa, and the household narrative that sprouts from it; it might have explored non-nuclear family units, or even just explored its host culture more deeply. In a podcast interview, the playwright states that he lived briefly in the Netherlands. Like Fiona and Alice, he had a primary identity that was tied to the UK, in his case attending a British school in the country.[18] I would not exactly want to hold someone's education against them—but this is a moment where a particular mode of private schooling seems to have limited a writer's ability to engage imaginatively with another place. Indeed, he cites the experiences of "friends I had at school"— not necessarily those who were gender transitioning—as providing the "experiences" on which he based part of the play.[19] I wanted a play addressing new ways of being alive among younger audiences to push harder against these traditions of family names, English self-understanding, and friends made at school.

Notes

1 Jon Brittain, *Rotterdam* (London: Methuen, 2015). All citations are to this edition and are provided parenthetically within the text.
2 See, for example, the account of theatres and urban renewal given in *Creative Tensions: Optimising the Benefits of Culture through Regeneration* (London: London Assembly, 2017).
3 Terri Paddock, "The Latest in Rotterdam's Extraordinary Trans Journey," *Terri Paddock* (podcast), June 29, 2017, www.terripaddock.com/rotterdam2017_podcast/.
4 Sophia Sleigh and Jonathan Prynn, "Covent Garden Entertainment Hub to Replace Arts Theatre after Eight-Year Battle," *The Evening Standard* (London), April 20, 2016, www.standard.co.uk/news/london/covent-garden-entertainment-hub-to-replace-arts-theatre-after-eightyear-battle-a3229521.html.
5 Ibid.
6 Cliff Joannou, editor of a gay listings magazine, noted that "The sense of Soho as a gay village or Vauxhall as a gay village is going," owing to rents. Ben Walters, "Closing Time for Gay Pubs—A New Victim of London's Soaring Property Prices," *The Guardian* (London), February 4, 2015, www.theguardian.com/society/2015/feb/04/closing-time-gay-pubs-lgbt-venues-property-prices.
7 Yas Necati, "*Summer in London* Is the Trans Play Actually Being Told by Transgender Actors," *The Independent* (London), July 25, 2017, www.independent.co.uk/

arts-entertainment/theatre-dance/summer-in-london-first-play-all-transgender-cast-uk-hir-rotterdam-representation-trans-stories-a7858806.html. Necati also takes issue with Fiona/Adrian being played by a cis actor.

8 Una Chaudhuri, *Staging Place: The Geography of Modern Drama* (Ann Arbor: University of Michigan Press, 1995), 10.

9 Matt Trueman, "Review: Rotterdam," *Whatsonstage.com*, July 29, 2016, www.whatsonstage.com/london-theatre/reviews/rotterdam-trafalgar-studios_41392.html.

10 Tim Bano, "Review: Rotterdam," *Time Out* (London), April 27, 2017.

11 Dominic Maxwell, "Theatre Review: Rotterdam at the Arts Theatre, WC2," *The Times* (London), 2017, www.thetimes.co.uk/article/theatre-review-rotterdam-at-the-arts-theatre-wc2-qwr9jcbm2.

12 Paddock, "The Latest in Rotterdam's Extraordinary Trans Journey."

13 A 2016 Guardian article suggests that some patients are waiting for as long as four years for appointments—something that would distort the timeframe of the play. Kezia Parkins, "Meet the Gender Reassignment Surgeons: 'Demand Is Going Through the Roof'," *The Guardian* (London), July 10, 2016, www.theguardian.com/society/2016/jul/10/meet-the-gender-reassignment-surgeons-demand-is-going-through-the-roof.

14 Bano, "Review: Rotterdam."

15 Sunny Drake, "Transitioning the Theatre Industry," *Canadian Theatre Review* 165 (Winter 2016): 55.

16 Ibid., 55–56.

17 "How Britain Voted," *Yougov.co.uk*, 2016, https://yougov.co.uk/news/2016/06/27/how-britain-voted/.

18 Qtd. in Paddock, "The Latest in Rotterdam's Extraordinary Trans Journey."

19 Ibid.

Works cited

Bano, Tim. "Review: Rotterdam." *Time Out* (London), April 27, 2017.

Brittain, Jon. *Rotterdam*. London: Methuen, 2015.

Chaudhuri, Una. *Staging Place: The Geography of Modern Drama*. Ann Arbor: University of Michigan Press, 1995.

Drake, Sunny. "Transitioning the Theatre Industry." *Canadian Theatre Review* 165 (Winter 2016): 55–9.

Maxwell, Dominic. "Theatre Review: Rotterdam at the Arts Theatre, WC2." *The Times* (London), 2017. www.thetimes.co.uk/article/theatre-review-rotterdam-at-the-arts-theatre-wc2-qwr9jcbm2.

Moore, Peter. "How Britain Voted." *Yougov.co.uk*, June 27, 2016. https://yougov.co.uk/news/2016/06/27/how-britain-voted/.

Necati, Yas. "Summer in London Is the Trans Play Actually Being Told by Transgender Actors." *The Independent* (London), July 25, 2017. www.independent.co.uk/arts-entertainment/theatre-dance/summer-in-london-first-play-all-transgender-cast-uk-hir-rotterdam-representation-trans-stories-a7858806.html.

Paddock, Terri. "The Latest in Rotterdam's Extraordinary Trans Journey." *Terri Paddock* (podcast), June 29, 2017. www.terripaddock.com/rotterdam2017_podcast/.

Parkins, Kezia. "Meet the Gender Reassignment Surgeons: 'Demand Is Going through the Roof'." *The Guardian* (London), July 10, 2016. www.theguardian.com/society/2016/jul/10/meet-the-gender-reassignment-surgeons-demand-is-going-through-the-roof.

Shah, Navin, Andrew Dismore, Shaun Bailey, Fiona Twycross, and Tony Devenish. *Creative Tensions: Optimising the Benefits of Culture through Regeneration*. London: London Assembly, 2017.

Sleigh, Sophia, and Jonathan Prynn. "Covent Garden Entertainment Hub to Replace Arts Theatre after Eight-Year Battle." *The Evening Standard* (London), April 20, 2016. www.standard.co.uk/news/london/covent-garden-entertainment-hub-to-replace-arts-theatre-after-eightyear-battle-a3229521.html.

Trueman, Matt. "Review: Rotterdam." *Whatsonstage.com*, July 29, 2016. www.whatsonstage.com/london-theatre/reviews/rotterdam-trafalgar-studios_41392.html.

Walters, Ben. "Closing Time for Gay Pubs—a New Victim of London's Soaring Property Prices." *The Guardian* (London), February 4, 2015. www.theguardian.com/society/2015/feb/04/closing-time-gay-pubs-lgbt-venues-property-prices.

4   Village feel

Deposit (2015), by Matt Hartley
Hampstead Theatre Downstairs, NW3 3EU
Saturday, 3 June 2017

The Devils (1961), by John Whiting
Royal Central School of Speech and Drama, NW3 3HY
Friday, 28 July 2017

Swiss Cottage is one of those Tube stops that make London's map promise experiences quainter than they turn out to be. Unlike at, say, Maida Vale or Chalk Farm, there actually is something that looks like a Swiss Cottage at this stop: this is Ye Olde Swiss Cottage, a mangy chain pub. The Cottage sits on a traffic island created by new motorways running around Hampstead Heath in the 1930s. Recent redevelopment in the area has proven controversial. In July 2015, the "Stop the Blocks!" campaign issued an "Open Letter" to Camden Council and developer A2Dominion, as part of a successful campaign to stop a new tower block nearby at 156 West End Lane. West Hampstead,

> with its multiple railway network interchange and widely touted "village feel" is also the focus of a series of large-scale developments approved by the council in spite of their impact on residents, their businesses and livelihoods and the area's heritage.[1]

Like the term "gentrification" itself, if without its critical bite, this use of "village feel" evoked an older understanding of English life.[2] Villages are local and intimate—places where people know their neighbours and look out for one another. It cuts other ways, of course: immigrants also don't live in villages, at least not in large numbers; they tend to move to welcoming cities, rather than to more closed communities. And villages are, finally, places where long-established hierarchies hold more sway: where a conventional order, from top to bottom, stays intact.

Regardless of your place on the political spectrum, some aspect of your side's politics is fanning the flames of London's real estate crisis. On the right, for example, there are subsidies for landlord-investors, a dislike of any form of rent control, antipathy to social housing, and general deregulation. The left is broadly more accepting of social housing, but far from immune to the language of "planning" and "sustainability" that can prevent further housing from being developed; its emphasis on grassroots activism, moreover, often agitates against new housing being built in areas like Swiss Cottage. A lot of individuals of all political bents, walks of life, class, and migration origins, have done spectacularly well by precipitous increases in property values—even if, collectively, the situation for renters and the dwindling number of state-supported housing residents has worsened.[3] And these individuals make their influence felt: not simply by voting, but by the culture they consume.

One of the most basic assumptions of theatre and performance history is that behaviours, attitudes, gestures, and dialogue can jump freely between social performance and theatrical performance. Do plays gain resonance by being performed in close proximity—in time, and in place? Can neighbourhoods accrete performativity, building up a communal (we might even say, a village) set or sense of concerns? And can performance in a particular neighbourhood at a particular time re-activate historical texts by refocusing and repurposing their concerns? I want to read two performances in Swiss Cottage—one of *Deposit* (2015) and one of *The Devils* (1962)—as a way of considering these questions. These performances organised the dignity of young adults around property relations. A housing environment deprived of public options—indeed even restricted in private development—massively favoured the interests of older, established people. This dynamic manifested in Swiss Cottage's theatres as a voyeuristic space for surveying the lives of the younger generations. London's generational inequality of property access played out in staging techniques: particularly, how the bodies of the young were made subject to the gaze of the more established.

There were a lot of property owners in the audience when I went to see *Deposit* at the Hampstead Theatre's downstairs space. That's not a guess or an assumption: it's what I overheard. The man sitting in front of me, who looked like a property developer, was a property developer; he was encouraging the other people in his party to buy more property. On the way out of this play about the terrible conditions endured by young aspirants to property owning in London, someone behind me said, "Thank god we don't have to worry about renting." This is the gauntlet you run even going out in London, these days: like the shouty newspapers, talk of property invades your space even when you don't want it to.

Growing from the 1960s theatre club celebrated in posters on its walls, the Hampstead Theatre has become one of the most important theatres in London, with an absolutely beautiful facility to match. They've grown large enough in fact to have a second stage. This Downstairs stage champions new writing, making it a good place to catch what people in London are worried about. And we are, simply put, scared out of our minds about real estate.

Deposit is not a particularly aesthetically accomplished play, but it is a vital one. It might even be accurate to say that its aesthetic reflects the abraded exhaustion of its characters. There are no lovely speeches and no striking turns of phrase.

Everyone is too tired for poetry. But it shows characters who, a generation or two ago, might have made such speeches, but are now simply too tired and ground down to do so, and further are surrounded by others too tired to listen. As a renter myself—as one of the deposit-scrambling classes—I spent most of *Deposit* clutched over in horror. The characters were precisely what I feared time in London was making me: the least interesting version of myself, flattened by the day-to-day exigencies of money-grubbing. None of them have outside interests, quirks, or really distinguishing characteristics, save the amount of money that they make. They talk incessantly about how they don't have time to do anything in London other than sit around, save, and hate themselves. The dramatis personae, even, describes everyone simply as name, age, occupation, and annual earnings: "RACHEL MAGUIRE, *twenty-nine, primary schoolteacher. 27K*"[4]

You walk into the Hampstead's downstairs space to find rows of pence pieces embedded into Lucite floorboards. The meaning is clear: money is embedded into every inch of the play's central flat.

> *Setting: A very, very small one-bedroom attic flat in a terraced house. Herne Hill, London. The flat consists of a bedroom, just big enough for a double bed. Adjoining is a lounge, slightly bigger, with no door. Off the corridor is a tiny kitchen and separate bathroom. But none of this has to be imagined realistically. The set should feel like a cage, a prison, a UFC fighting ring, a zoo enclosure. Throughout the play, the space that the flat is imagined in should shrink until it barely exists.*

The Ultimate Fighting Championship, or UFC, offers a less rule-bound version of professional boxing, undertaken of course at greater risk to the participants. *Deposit* suggests that Millennial life in general is like this: the same form of contest that our parents went through, only less regulated and with more to lose. And we're all in each other's arena: freed of older generations' taboos, perhaps, but without any space to indulge in them. Part of Londoners' seeming worldliness may just be that we all spend time amidst the bodily functions of others: there's no longer any room for daintiness.

The precise address is Flat 3, 7 Kestrel Avenue, a real-world location. While areas of the city like Shoreditch and Hackney have seen an incursion of middle-class people into what had previously been predominantly working-class areas, Herne Hill, which started life as a Victorian suburb, has always been for middle-class families. The play tracks the slow subdivision of acceptable middle-class space, as the dwellings professionals can afford grow smaller and smaller. Many of the neighbourhood's terraced houses, each designed for single families (and, to be fair, their servants) have been subdivided into different units. For this, *Deposit*'s characters are paying £1,742/month. Here, frankly, the playwright seems to be tightening the screws a little bit. A quick online search suggests that they're being ripped off for a one-bedroom (much less a tiny one) in Herne Hill.[5] Nevertheless the amount expresses the gap between London's punishing rental market and its slightly less-punishing property market. Ownership does not so much resonate as blare within these characters' minds. It is nearly everything they think of.

This small apartment updates the onstage house in English theatre. A self-contained family home was the iconic basic unit of nineteenth-century theatre. Post-war plays track the division of Victorian homes into smaller units, with obvious state-of-the-nation implications. John Obsborne's *Look Back in Anger* (1956), for example, makes much of the inability of working-class intellectual Jimmy to live amidst the cramped surroundings of an attic flat. Terence Rattigan's characters often face down the dread of having to live in places like (heavens) Earls Court. Contemporary theatre-goers face this cognitive dissonance when watching these older plays. You mentally adjust for what would have been unthinkable at the time—humans reduced to animals by living in Archway or Kentish Town—and coo accordingly, marvelling at the human spirit. You then return to your seven flatmates in Harrow.

Deposit reveals housing anxiety being classed downwards. Living in cramped conditions has always been normal in London for those outside of the professional classes. "House in Multiple Occupation"—for a dwelling in which multiple households share some facilities within a single structure—is the modern-day term for this kind of arrangement, when legally licenced. Unlicenced arrangements, like the one depicted in the play, are of course also quite common, particularly among new immigrants to the city and country. There's nothing new about them—except, it's implied, for those with middle-class jobs, and the implied sensibilities that go with them.

Deposit's four characters, two hetero couples (Ben and Rachel, Sam and Melanie), have decided to live together for one year in order to "save money for a deposit," that is, to be put up as part of a mortgage. If you live in London right now, you will hear this expression over and over again until it worms its way into your very soul. It has an iconic quality: it suggests you are on the path to respectability, which in contemporary England usually means property ownership. Over the course of a year, *Deposit* shows these characters getting on worse and worse, until hostilities break out. In this, the play gets at some of what it's actually like to live in London right now without generous parents and/or a non-corporate salary. All of the characters have solidly middle-class jobs: teacher, press secretary, PR agent, and doctor. The men are the characters Jimmy in *Look Back* aspired to be: they have gone to university, have careers, and are in settled relationships. Yet they are falling through the cracks in contemporary society, at least as they imagine them; and rapidly aging into catastrophe, at least as they understand it. In the script, Matt's age is given as 30; on the night that I saw it, he had been bumped up to 36, making his plight all the more desperate within that calculus of age-to-earnings-to-friends-making-partner-at-their-law-firm that we're all so familiar with.

The Victorian middle classes' ascent into single-family dwellings was imagined around the separation of bodily functions. The Freudian revolution of course sought to unpack this, showing how sexual desire sloshes out of our attempts to keep it neatly packaged. The extremely close quarters of this apartment shows the Victorian separations collapsing back into themselves, while the characters themselves are too tired to have sex: "BEN. Sleep? You're being polite. It's like we're setting up a dogging site." Dogging is an echt-English form of public sex, in which strangers watch a couple having intercourse in a public place. As the name suggests, dogging has all manner of unpleasant, slightly grotty associations: it's a lower-class activity, at least in its readiest associations. And in fact the performance itself has elements of being like the "dogging site." We do watch the couples simulate sex with one another, albeit mimed and under blankets. Yet unlike cultural products from earlier, more free-swinging eras—a Hanif Kureishi novel, for example—there was no suggestion in the play that I saw of an erotic frisson, either among the couples or between the couples and the audience. Sex is simply another bodily function hindered by the too-close proximity of other people.

All of this happens in the shadow of incredible wealth. Rachel, pointing to one of the windows, notes that "If you bend, peer out, you can see the Shard." From where I write this in an attic in Tottenham, I can see the Shard, too. For much of the city of London, its unattainable real estate becomes an everyday symbol of how far your reality falls short of what the city can offer—given unlimited wealth, of course. Still, you make your allowances:

Ben: It's going to be great. Remember, this is not for ever.
Rachel: It's a chapter.

Ben and Rachel espouse the belief, shared by everyone in the play, that temporary privations are simply part of what one makes do with in order to climb onto the so-called property ladder. They are the cause and the product of the perfect storm creating this problem: they will not leave the market, nor will they agitate for it to be changed. They don't have time; imagining a comprehensive solution to the London housing market feels more like science fiction than science fiction does. None of these characters are particularly beneficent people, at least in their home life: though they might work with children, as teachers or doctors, they clearly need all of what grace they possess for their time at work.

This is a great play for circular thinking. At no point does anyone in the play question the wisdom of ultimately buying a place. For all of the characters, living in London is simply the only thing one does, the only possibility of living a feasible life. In a play mostly bereft of long speeches, Ben is given a lengthy one about the apparent alternatives:

Ben: . . . . It's. God. Ahhh. I've just, well, I've found the last few days rather depressing. Stevenage. Bloody Stevenage. Well, it's not Stevenage per se. Places like that, Aldershot, Crawley, you know those places you normally go by on a high-speed train and don't understand why anyone would want to get off there? Oh god the look of them. Flat. Spawning identikit houses for miles. Culturally bereft. Geographically insipid. . . . The only reason for those places is because people can't go any further from London. Everyone spends their life in trains or in the car. So the people who live there become zombies. And that's why my brother has become. And my brother, I can't say it really in any other way, is, was kind of my hero. He played drums in a band.

Rachel chimes in: "Try finding history on every corner of Stevenage, you fucking can't, it's just Greggs or charity shops." Circular thinking, with catastrophes on each side, is of course what the world looks like in the midst of the years-long mania that life in London occasionally feels like. London is unaffordable but the outside of London is death but London is unaffordable; around and around we go. Of course, none of the play's characters seem particularly far away from being "zombies" themselves, as anything that makes them interesting—any hobbies or, frankly, personality—is stripped away from them.

Unspoken in the play, but everywhere, is its rigidity of a new class structure. This is not *Downton Abbey*—there are no servants or other well-established historical signposts. Yet these characters, too, are trapped, albeit within a very different set of assumptions. Whereas the unthinkable dilemmas of the turn of the century might involve bringing lower-class money into the family, here the characters see in the suburbs only the downmarket bakeries and used-clothing stores that would mark them as having fallen below their appropriate level of cultural capital. Ben and Rachel make slightly less money than Sam and Melanie, but cannot quite bring themselves to economise, for example, by shopping in discount stores ("I know what fucking Poundland is, Mel."). They are stuck in the middle-class downward mobility of their generation—if not in terms of jobs, then in terms of the opportunities for privacy and meaningful fulfilment that those jobs can provide. Like the best horror stories, the play shows characters unable to remove themselves from a particular place and mindset.

Worrying about their own situation totally isolates these characters from the rest of the world. There is no discussion of anyone else who is struggling. Where other people appear, it is entirely in terms of their humblebragging presence on social media:

Melanie: Oh my god, have you seen that Claire Anderson has got engaged?
Rachel: How could I not, it's all over Facebook. Flashing that huge, obscene ring, whilst in that tropical paradise. It's so shameless.

The tropics mentioned second-hand in an aside about Facebook is the only time the play moves outside of London. Made from this locked-in vantage point, these comments demonstrate a noxious aloneness that is very 2017. No one mentions politics, although all work for one arm of the state or another. We never see them read newspapers; their only awareness of the wider world seems to be through social media. They are busy—frantically busy—and constantly tired; Sam, for example, laments that "This rotation I am on seems never-ending." In the staging

I saw the characters were two hetero couples, but this play could work in precisely the same way with two couples of any sexual orientation: gay or straight, they would have the same problems. Difficult economic circumstances have ground them down to near-interchangeability.

While they save, they drink. As the two couples sell themselves on living with friends, they note that is a chance to party without going out ("My poor liver. Is this what the year ahead looks like?!") This is far from the first generation of Londoners to make do with the recompenses of alcohol. But the play is one of the most accurate representations of our era's routine lubrication of awful social circumstances by prosecco. Premium alcohols realise social ambitions that otherwise can't be met. The only precisely defined prop in the play is "*a bottle of El Jimador, silver*"—a tequila brand owned by Brown-Forman, one of the largest American alcohol conglomerates. And alcohol is the only thing that makes the characters happy. In Matt's case it permits the return of "the Beast," the drunken (and presumably more interesting) person he was when he met his partner in university. Getting "completely Winehoused" allows them to briefly return to being full-fledged human beings; their days and weekends are punctuated with routine hangovers. The Amy Winehouse route, cultural capital and even adequate housing acquired through liver destruction, is preferable to a more placid life in the suburbs.

All onstage are spinning in air, unsupported by family and unvisited by friends. Biological relationships manifest entirely as something you can inherit money from. The year's gap between publication and second performance is again interesting: in the 2015 version of the play, Sam inherits £40,000; when I saw it a year and a half later, this amount had been raised to £60,000. Here again Sam speaks in pure exposition, like the language of his own Wikipedia entry: "He moved to Canada when I was very young. He wanted a better life. He wanted me and Mum to come with him. We didn't. He got hit by a drunk driver." These present-day Londoners are too busy to worry about the rest of England, much less the rest of the world. Overseas money will simply help Sam to buy, becoming part of the vast influxes of foreign capital holding London's property market aloft. Nothing is ever made again of this uncle; certainly his notion of moving elsewhere to secure a "better life" never enters the thinking of any of these characters. Instead, the happy accident of a Winnipeg traffic fatality means that Sam and Melanie can start looking for a property immediately. They do, securing a £500,000 place in nearby Lordship Lane.

Where was the audience in all of this? Assembled around the arena in which these young people thrash out this unpleasant year of their lives, it's hard not to feel voyeuristic—like we'd actually paid for that dogging site. We are getting to have an experience none of the play's characters get to have. Melanie asks, "What is the point of living in London if you don't get to experience its delights, eh?" None of them can, for example, afford to go to the theatre. They are being made into people whose only joy in life will come in property ownership. Given that theatre audiences skew older and more settled, I wondered if the uncomfortable-looking sort-of-young man in the second room, bent over in evident discomfort, added to the evening's spectacle: another one of the property-less damned. I could no more figure out a way out of the play's dilemmas than those onstage.

As the evening wore on, *Deposit* felt increasingly like a projection of my own most basic fears about my life in London, staged for the benefit of those in a stabler position. Sam, finally, emerges as the play's most negative character. He describes himself as the product of a hardscrabble background who has made something of himself. He reveals, in the process, a habit of speaking in rehearsed soundbites: "Yes. At secondary school I excelled at sciences. I was told it was irrelevant. That no doctors were ever created at my school." Sam pulled himself up, to the point where he has become a junior doctor—making enough money to save more than Ben and Rachel. Early on in their time together, Sam and Melanie inadvertently reveal that they are saving much more than the £10,000 Ben and Rachel have planned to save for the year. The couples' relationship never recovers and descends into bickering. Growing increasingly exasperated with Ben, Sam finally gives him a wince-inducing lecture in basic economics: "Somebody has to say this to you. Earn more money if that is what you desire. Work harder for it or choose a new line of work." Sam kicks Ben when he's down—he is the play's most egregious character, in terms of his contributions to dialogue. Yet, in the world outside of the apartment, he's some sort of children's doctor; his public contribution is unquestionable. Like all of the other characters, Sam simply can't wrangle his professional status into any sort of recompensatory home life. As in the UFC, he needs to win against someone, and Ben is simply the most conveni-ent target. Under different circumstances, these characters might get on with each other—or, ideally, never have to live together.

The crux of the play's dilemma is that Sam and Melanie seek to leave their lease arrangement with the other couple early, causing financial issues for Ben and Rachel. The play's more substantial issue is the seeming arbitrariness of fortune for the contemporary middle classes: it's finally not professional status but inherit-ance that allows Sam and Melanie to potentially attain what they want. Talent is secondary to what your family can give you. In his own mind Sam has pulled him-self up by his bootstraps, but few in contemporary London can own by bootstraps alone. All of these characters would know people working in the corporate sector, and their non-appearance in the play is not accidental: they simply wouldn't live like this, nor would they have to.

This year in the flat shreds each one of them in a slightly different way. Sam and Melanie break up; he takes his deposit and leaves. Following the breakup of their relationship, Melanie moves to Bristol. The play's one grace note is Ben and Rachel embracing at the end, their relationship (if not necessarily their ownership dreams) having survived. But some grace note: what awaits them is more cohabi-tation, more sacrifice, and finally no doubt some desperate leap onto the property market. There are no alternatives.

And this seeming inevitability is reflected, finally, in the play itself. The play's characters are unhappy about their situation, but this unhappiness has no specific target. The homeowners of *Yerma* (chapter six), who already own their house, mention Boris Johnson and Sadiq Kahn, the current and former mayors of London, by name: they're au courant with politics, and informed about their rights. In contrast, the characters in *Deposit* turn their anger on each other: on their friends, but also into their own relationships. What survives is one of the play's proto-family units: the long-standing couple of Ben and Rachel. By the end of the play, there is no common cause uniting these friends into something like a society. There are only individual families, one of which survives and one of which fails.

Three months later, I found myself back in Swiss Cottage. I had returned effectively for theatrical bird-watching, a chance to see something rare. Drama schools will often put on historical plays requiring large casts—they're one of the best ways to see Restoration Comedy, for example, performed with anything like routine frequency. Tonight's bird was rarer still: John Whiting's *The Devils* (1961), performed across the street from the Hampstead at the Royal Central School of Speech and Drama by their MA Acting (Classical) students. *The Devils* was not something I ever thought I would see onstage: an early 1960's play, it was commissioned by the Royal Shakespeare Company under Peter Hall, and later made into a Ken Russell film. It originates from a period when explicit sexuality was starting to appear on British stages. The play's gender politics are, we might say, of its era. Sexual repression turns women into devils, leading ultimately to the destruction of a male sensualist by a tyrannical state; it concludes with a nun pleasuring herself with her dead antagonist's shinbone.

The past 60 years' UK politics have largely supported what would have seemed liberatory sexuality in 1961, without following through on other sorts of political rights, particularly those relating to state support. The basic right to extra-marital sex among the non-policed classes—those affluent enough to afford what a dominant neoliberalism considers "normal"—is no longer a primary political issue. Within the broadest public discourse the consumption of sexuality has never been more accepted, while the support of humans engaged in those activities continues to waver. On the one hand, 2016 had presented Crispin Blunt, a Tory MP, advocating in Parliament for his right to continue using amyl nitrate, or "poppers"—precisely the drug that Derek Jarman's punk-rock squat dweller in *Jubilee* (1978) was named for.[6] (I address the 2018 theatrical re-staging of that piece, briefly, in the introduction.) Blunt's advocacy of a drug primarily associated with sexual enhancement among gay men spoke to a frankness and acceptance of sexual practices that would have been prosecuted and condemned even a relatively short time ago. Gay marriage was legalised under a Conservative government. On the other hand, every category of social support for those harmed by sexual practices—from migrants to rape victims to sex workers—has been the victim of austerity-era policies. As Lesley Hall notes, the ways that the untroubled discourse of mainstream sexuality has both greatly widened what is permissive while increasing inequalities within whose rights are supported and whose neglected.[7]

I have tracked throughout this project what I term *exhausted radicalism and the hedonistic body:* the way that the stage currently endorses a kind of normalised extremeness in its depiction of sexuality, while excluding or minimising other dimensions of politics. Anyway, *The Devils* in 2017 was an established enough part of the cultural heritage that those classes it had been initially designed to shock could attend unreservedly. The audience that night seemed solidly familial: people brought their parents, siblings, that kind of thing. Multiple generations of formidable-looking North Londoners milled about purposefully, coolly apprais-ing the situation. Lapsed colonial that I am, I felt intimidated, in that way that I always do around too thick a cluster of middle-class Britons. This audience was full of terrifyingly well-put-together people of all ages. (I mean, *scarves*.) If these people had asked me to fetch drinks, I would probably have done so. In my imagination, all of them were homeowners—the sort who passed along deposits, and even the occasional apartment, to their kids.

Sociology supports my class intimidation. A 2016 survey of the performing arts in England found that 73% of actors were from middle-class backgrounds, despite these backgrounds making up only 29 percent of the overall population.[8] As the survey notes, this "class inequality is particularly problematic in acting because of the way in which the profession is tied to cultural industries, such as theatre, television and film, whose cultural outputs shape and organise understandings of society."[9] The study confirms all of your worst suspicions about affluent young people in the arts:

> Tommy, for example, was from a very wealthy background and had attended an elite public school. He explained that he initially quit acting in his mid-20s after sustained periods of unemployment but after a long period travelling had recently re-entered the profession. . . . Andy, whose parents are both cli-nicians, explained that his existence as an actor is heavily contingent on the ability to 'call mum' during lean spells for financial top-ups.[10]

Attending one of the " 'Big 4' London drama schools"—of which Central is one—was seen as key to a career.[11] I was, in other words, seeing actors whose London visibility meant they had a leg up on those from elsewhere in the country.

And I was seeing a lot of them indeed. There's nothing particularly new or noteworthy about stage nudity in London—it hasn't been truly shocking, at least in and of itself, for 50 years. From the vantage point of 1961, when it was first performed, *The Devils* was clearly trying to fight for some of the new sexual freedoms and bodily openness. The lead character, Father Grandier, is a human-ist libertine. The village's establishment is already on the side of the fulfilment of sexual urges, at least when gossiping to one another. Mannoury and Adam, respectively, the town's surgeon and chemist, get things off to a fruitily historical start. The "things" Grandier gets up to, for example, with the Widow Ninon, are on everyone's lips:

Mannoury: Don't gape. Things said and things done.
Adam: By the priest? Yes, I've heard.

. . .

They look at NINON

Mannoury: I've attended her. Medically.

Adam: Have you?

Mannoury: It's not widowhood gives that contentment. That walk.[12]

The men leer constantly at women's bodies while remarking on their satiating qualities. A Sewerman sets out his philosophy of life:

> And what makes a man happy? To eat, and set the drains awash. To sit in the sun and ferment the rubbish. To go home, and find comfort in his wife's conduit. Then why should I feel ashamed or out of place down here?

Whiting's women themselves are conduits and swinging hips, on offer like a turkey leg at a Renaissance Faire. Religion is either a manifestation of repression or politically expeditious way of removing dangerous people from positions of influence.

Father Grandier advocates for a theology of free love that will acknowledge what the Sewerman claims: that people should embrace the bodily aspects of their nature. His antagonist is the hunchbacked Sister Jeanne des Anges. After Grandier rebuffs her sublimated sexual advances, Jeanne seeks revenge by claiming to be possessed by devils. Much business follows: shouting in Latin, some confessions of demonic carnality ("She says that she and her sisters were compelled to form themselves into an obscene altar, and were worshipped"), and finally a staged orgy, the nuns offering themselves to the townspeople who flood onstage to watch.

The play's advocacy of sexual consumption is matched with an indifference to its female victims.[13] Grandier's seduction of the teenage girl Phillippe, for example, which takes place in the confessional, is described thusly by the stage directions: "*GRANDIER comes out from the box: compassion*" (34). The town's women are reciprocally unsubtle in embracing this compassion. Phillippe, for example, whom Grandier is hired to instruct, reports that

> In the early hours of the morning . . . my bedroom is suffocatingly hot. . . . I've asked them to take away the velvet curtains . . . my thoughts fester . . . and yet they are so tender . . . my body . . . Father . . . my body . . . I wish to be touched.

(33)

Grandier is, in his own account, as trapped in his body as everyone else is: "O God, O my God, my God! Release me! Free me! These needs! Have mercy" (18). Yet after Phillippe announces her pregnancy, Phillippe almost literally—to use the twenty-first-century term—ghosts her: "How can I help you? Take my hand There. Like touching the dead, isn't it? Goodbye, Phillippe" (62). The play remains remorselessly on Grandier's side, ennobling his sexual experimentation and eventual suffering for it by turning him a Christ figure.

While all of this was unfolding, two seats over in the audience, a young woman was growing increasingly agitated. I was surprised: part of the game of theatre-going is keeping cool regardless of what is being presented onstage. "This is so stupid," she kept saying, to anyone who would listen. "I don't know why this is happening." I was genuinely very close to correcting her—to tell her to be quiet, to leave; that this was Serious Theatre. About ten seconds before I said anything, she jumped up on stage to join the townspeople onstage, shouting and writhing and generally carrying on, before being driven off by black-helmeted guards. She had been a plant! I had completely fallen for it.

Rather than by audience intervention, the orgy is broken up by one Prince Henri De Conde, who arrives claiming that the holy relic he has in a box can remove the demonic presence. The nuns knock it off in the presence of "A phial of the blood of our Lord Jesus Christ"; this turns out to be empty (78). De Conde reveals that the proceedings were at best psychological nonsense—clearly there are no actual devils—but then allows the proceedings to continue for their sheer political expedience in bringing Grandier down.

The orgiastic spectacles created by the nuns' possessions, or indeed by Grandier's execution for denying the will of the state, will not change anything. The state is an elite conspiracy against right-minded individualists; Grandier would ideally have been allowed to continue tending his sexual garden unmolested. We observe in this thread of Whiting's writing that aspect of the late 1960s counterculture-to-be that would become part of our contemporary state's emphasis on privatisation. If the state is invasive, intrusive, and opposed to individualism, a rational response would be to de-fund it at once. And, on this austerity-era stage, we lived with the evolution of this kind of thinking. State institutions had not been entirely de-funded, but a certain level of buy-in was now required to fully access them, to support (for example) the kind of arts career that would make good on this sort of education.

The Devils in 2017 presented a victory lap against the prosecution of extramarital heterosexual sex: the recapitulation of a victory that has already occurred. It also gave a proleptic version of that lack of support for sexuality's victims, those whose lives are destroyed by it, that is also apparent in our current moment. The moment most calculated to shock was the audience plant interrupting the performance, rather than the performance itself. Whiting's play was no longer a piece of social criticism; indeed, its attitudes allowed for a certain amount of mere social reproduction. As is often the case with canonical drama, the society it had originally critiqued—the bourgeois it had sought to épater—had adjusted to what it was saying, enveloping its message into general acceptance.

Forty years on, we live in a time of a sexual freedom largely unimaginable to the general population of 1961. Historical progress is not à la carte. But it's also possible to see in *The Devils* the beginning of the imagination of the state as the enemy—as a factor to be reined in and curtailed so that the individual might thrive. Four years later, Edward Bond's *Saved* (1965)—which showed lower-class people living in social housing—would similarly show the state tamping down the individual's inclinations, in that case leading to the famed violence of its pram-stoning scene, where a circle of working-class youths murder a baby. The point of so many plays from the sixties was that our lower, baser, violent, libidinal energies needed to be unleashed from society's control over them—presented, of course, by theatres like the Royal Shakespeare Company (RSC) that enjoyed a high level of state subsidy. This occasionally, however, extended into an attack on the state more generally. The defunding bargain that evolved from this has allowed subsidised state structures—drama schools, the opera, the RSC—to remain, but most readily for members of the middle classes able to self-subsidise in one way or another. The formidable resources of the state remain available, but only to those who are able to afford the buy-in.

The Devils gives its most trenchant opportunities for self-representation to the main male sexual libertine, played in this production (as in the original) by a white man. In a tableau, Grandier, before being stripped to be tortured and killed, "*stands looking long and deeply at his reflection*" in a mirror he holds. No other actor in the play was allowed such a moment; no other character's mind comes so close to the surface. Unlike the female characters, often naked and always in group arrangements, Grandier is given the greatest freedom to show himself as both an individual body and a soul.

My sympathy here was with the student performers against the opportunities they were given. But *The Devils*, performed at this moment in this setting, seemed to substantiate what *Deposit* critiqued: the expression of a society giving its greatest opportunities to its settled classes. The restaging of the play in this particular place had brought into clearer relief some themes present from its first performance: most prominently, its fear of the egalitarian tastes of the crowd. The themes of the play flattered the sensibilities of the neighbourhood. It concluded with the triumph of the powers that be: the state victorious over Grandier; the mob pacified by bringing down the free-thinking individualist, but with the baseline lecherousness of the town presumably proceeding. The masses who flooded the stage were like the new residents the "Stop the Blocks!" organisation feared: obstreperous presences changing the nature of the village, bodies rendered threatening because there were too many of them in one place.

Taken together—staged across the street from one another, during an overlapping period of time—these two plays reflected on a wider lack of progressive possibility on the present-day London stage. In the end, the Millennials of *Deposit* have either each other and an insufficient deposit; half of them don't even have that. And the students actors in *The Devils* were left fighting a battle against a morality that had been defeated 50-odd years before. In this neighbourhood resistant to build spaces for new people, these two plays showed the mindset of a world where older people are not only firmly in charge—holding the property—but also dominant over what topics are discussed, and what cultural battles are significant.

Generational disparity means control: not simply of property, but of what sort of life-narratives the younger generation gets to embody. As in *Deposit*, some will be given gifts, while others won't be: the dignity of the younger generation is the older's to distribute. And *The Devils* offered an older generation's idea of what young people should be fighting for: an understanding of sexual freedoms that we more or less take for granted, which in its way forecloses the newer and more challenging forms of sexual identity that are now emerging. In performance as in housing policy, change in the village seemed far off.

Notes

1 "Press Release: Open Letter to Camden Council & A2Dominion," *Save West Hampstead*, July 31, 2015, https://savewesthampstead.wordpress.com/2015/07/31/press-release-open-letter-to-camden-council-a2dominion/.
2 I describe the term's origins and class connotations in my first chapter.
3 So, for example, as James Rosbrook-Thompson and Gary Armstrong note, "By purchasing their property and selling during 'booms' in the housing market, enterprising residents of estates situated in prime locations stood to make tens of thousands and, if they were particularly lucky and held their nerve, hundreds of thousands of pounds" (*Mixed-Occupancy Housing in London: A Living Tapestry* [London: Palgrave Macmillan, 2018], 3).
4 Matt Hartley, *Deposit* (Nick Hern Books, 2015), www.dramaonlinelibrary.com:443/plays/deposit-iid-158513/do-9781784602697-div-00000009, https://doi.org/10.5040/9781784602697.00000002. All citations are to this unpaginated edition.
5 "To Rent," *Zoopla.com*, August 19, 2017, www.zoopla.co.uk/.
6 Frances Perraudin, "Tory MP Crispin Blunt: 'I Out Myself as Poppers User'," *The Guardian*, 2016, www.theguardian.com/politics/2016/jan/20/tory-mp-crispin-blunt-poppers-drug-policy.
7 Lesley A. Hall, *Sex, Gender, and Social Change in Britain since 1880*, 2nd ed. (New York: Palgrave Macmillan, 2013).
8 Sam Friedman, Dave O'Brien, and Daniel Laurison, "'Like Skydiving without a Parachute': How Class Origin Shapes Occupational Trajectories in British Acting," *Sociology* 51, no. 5 (2016): 997.
9 Ibid., 993.
10 Ibid., 1000.
11 Ibid., 1002.
12 John Whiting, *The Devils* (New York: Hill and Wang, 1961), 7. All further citations are given parenthetically in the text.
13 Thanks Sebastian Lecourt for this phrasing.

Works cited

Friedman, Sam, Dave O'Brien, and Daniel Laurison. "'Like Skydiving without a Parachute': How Class Origin Shapes Occupational Trajectories in British Acting." *Sociology* 51, no. 5 (2016): 992–1010.

Hall, Lesley A. *Sex, Gender, and Social Change in Britain since 1880*. 2nd ed. New York: Palgrave Macmillan, 2013.

Hartley, Matt. *Deposit*. Nick Hern Books, 2015. https://doi.org/10.5040/9781784602697.00000002.

Perraudin, Frances. "Tory MP Crispin Blunt: 'I Out Myself as Poppers User'." *The Guardian*, January 20, 2016. www.theguardian.com/politics/2016/jan/20/tory-mp-crispin-blunt-poppers-drug-policy.

"Press Release: Open Letter to Camden Council & A2dominion." *Save West Hampstead*, July 31, 2015. https://savewesthampstead.wordpress.com/2015/07/31/press-release-open-letter-to-camden-council-a2dominion/.

Rosbrook-Thompson, James, and Gary Armstrong. *Mixed-Occupancy Housing in London: A Living Tapestry*. London: Palgrave Macmillan, 2018.

"To Rent." *Zoopla.com*, August 19, 2017. www.zoopla.co.uk/.

Whiting, John. *The Devils*. New York: Hill and Wang, 1961.

5   Croydon versus the world

Malteaser threesomes and entrepreneurial sweatshirts in the shadow of Grenfell

White Rabbit Red Rabbit **(2011) and** *Blank* **(2015) by Nassim Soleimanpour**
The Bush Theatre, 7 Uxbridge Rd, Shepherd's Bush, London W12 8LJ
11–16 September 2017

The audience volunteer's black sweatshirt at the Iranian playwright's interactive drama read CROYDON VS THE WORLD. That's the sort of moment guides to London's diversity like to savour: local signifiers, international impact, provocatively branded streetwear. To quote its maker, the sweatshirt "Let the World Know That Croydon Is in the House," a small design house asserting the presence of the feisty and diverse South London neighbourhood in the global imaginary.[1] London eagerly asserts itself as a place of strivers who have fought to get here. "London remains," Tim Butler notes, "as it has been for hundreds of years, the capital city attracting those who do not fit into their home-towns and villages across the nation"—and, indeed, the world.[2] Striving implies a continual fight for a deserved success, and even survival. But who makes it, and who doesn't? Since the 2010 coalition government, UK immigration—even for purposes of family unification—has been tied to income levels. Indeed, the only category of UK migrant visa whose monetary requirements decreased in the last ten years was the Tier 1 (Entrepreneur) visa.[3] The new migrant, like the new citizen, was to be scrappy, self-directed, and asking nothing from the state. This chapter addresses how even avowedly progressive theatre interested in migrant voices could encourage its audiences to consider citizenship—their own and those of others—within these terms.

In August 2017, the Bush Theatre in Shepherd's Bush, West London, put on a four-play festival of the works of Iranian playwright Nassim Soleimanpour, with the playwright himself in attendance. These plays invited audiences to consider the freedoms they enjoyed living in a state where freedom of expression is not restricted. I want to talk about what it means to advocate for an entrepreneurial vision of migration in the summer of the nearby Grenfell Tower fires, when the issue of who constitutes, and who should be added to, the UK population was particularly fraught and critical. The festival revealed how difficult it was to imagine contemporary citizenship—much less migration—outside of a paradigm of private ownership over one's self, property, and talent.

Soleimanpour became a literal *cause celebre* for his first play, *White Rabbit, Red Rabbit* (2011, hereinafter *WRRR*). Initially unable to travel out of Iran because of his refusal to perform mandatory military service, Soleimanpour simply mailed his script to a variety of theatre companies and actors. The website for Nassim's plays lists the celebrities who have been involved in these performances: Nathan Lane, Ken Loach, John Hurt, and Whoopi Goldberg. Celebrity participation encouraging audience interaction also means that the script is a sort of net, scooping up whatever local idiosyncrasies the local performer wants to add. In the ensuing few years, Soleimanpour had been able to get out of military service. He was around the theatre this week, appearing in *Nassim*, another cold actor-read piece, and appearing in the theatre bar after performances.

It's not surprising that theatre written by someone evading the heavy burdens of an intrusive state might propose special rights for the exceptional individual. However, the context of these plays in their recent London performance is different from that in which they were written. In this chapter I describe how the improvisatory nature of Soleimanpour's performances let us study how *class capture* can inform audience improvisation as well as formal scripts. Presented by celebrities, these scripts frame their discussion about migration within a city's pre-existing sense of what it means to have succeeded. Although Soleimanpour could not have known about the Arts Council's requirement of reflecting an audience when he wrote his plays, they nevertheless cohere with that agenda. They give a framework of provocative generalities for the performers to massage into an ultimately reassuring rhetoric for their audiences. They let us self-fashion as good, entrepreneurial subjects, too.

It's easy to describe the Grenfell victims without particularity. Not all of the residents were migrants—although, as Mark Rice-Oxley notes, "more than half the adult victims had arrived in the country since 1990."[4] Grenfell was not, Rice-Oxley concludes, "a microcosm of Britain or London. There were few white-collar workers among the victims and only seven white Britons, indicative of how the disaster disproportionately affected minority ethnic communities."[5] Their predominant uniting element was that they lived in state-supported housing, that the sector had been defunded over decades, and that they died as a result of that lack of funding. (Indeed as I write this, underfunding to the sector of people requiring care seems likely to be the primary cause of coronavirus deaths, which once again are impacting the elderly and minority ethnic communities disproportionately.[6]) They were people who fit into a category of person the state no longer funded— often, in multiple categories of undesirability.

I focus here on the *Nassim Plays* because they worked within our era's dominant narratives about migration and citizenship. Specifically, they present migrants as people who have eluded an intrusive government—who have eluded state support, rather than require it. That these plays were written in another country, and for an unspecified world audience, suggests how widely held these beliefs about government are worldwide. Many plays addressed migrant experiences in London theatre during this period.[7] Soleimanpour's plays depict migrants self-styling as entrepreneurial—as state policy forcibly encourages, for both migrants and settled populations alike.

1 *Blank* (11 September 2017)

Our performer for *Blank* was Mel Giedroyc, formerly a host of the *Great British Bake Off* before the latter show's departure from the state-owned BBC to the private-but-also-ultimately-state-owned Channel 4. In this performance, the local details the script invited Mel to share nearly overwhelmed the piece itself. Mel came on wearing a pantsuit, which she introduced as not really age-appropriate— she had acquired it at Forever 21, a mall clothing store aimed as its name suggests at younger people. Before she really got down to business, she gave us some details about the Bake Off, about which she declined to say anything negative. It was hard not to feel charmed and welcomed by her utterly professional, utterly charming schtick. Going back to the music hall and beyond, performers like her have helped people feel at home in London: not only welcomed but also driven along by a forceful, inveigling personality. Equally, though, hers was mimetic irony: reinforcing and reconstructing the city's own sense of place, making it familiar, rather than challenging it. The ostensibly 70-minute play took about two hours to perform.

According to the script, *Blank* requires only "[a] copy of this play . . . two chairs . . . a table . . . 60 blank sheets of paper . . . a board . . . tools to affix paper to the board . . . a thick marker pen."[8] This could be run in the smallest fringe theatre or seminar room, requiring minimal commitment from everyone involved. As Rosabel Tan writes, "By stripping the play of rehearsals, the audience gets to share the process of discovery with the one person they're never allowed to share it with: the actor."[9] The actor is not supposed to have any prior knowledge. The script makes up for this by, frankly, being a bit controlling. The actor is told to

> [s]tand and sit while you read. Standing may be better. Move around if you want to. . . . Do your best to keep eye contact with the audience. Sometimes this will be difficult—but try. Don't let this slow you down, though! Pace is important. Don't let the audience get ahead of us!
>
> (np)

These scripts in reading, as well as these plays in performance, often involve unstable power relations: attempts at control made between the actor and the audience, or between playwright and actor.

These plays also in effect line the audience up against the often-adversarial performer—but then, most of the time, bring the two sides together, engineering a consensus. As a reviewer of one production of Soleimanpour's plays in Edinburgh noted, "much depended on the actor having faith in the words in front of them and wanting them to succeed—a cynical performer could destroy the performance."[10]

But of course such a performer would be incentivised against doing so. Everyone in our audience, for example, had paid £20—or thereabouts—to be there. Most of the time, these scripts create a self-fulfilling good feelings machine: the audience wants them to succeed because we've both paid for it and been asked to contribute directly to its success. Even if the interactions are simple—saying a number when prompted, considering going up on stage—all audience members play some part. The scripts invite us to feel as though we're on the threshold of direct participation—even if, for the most part, we remain safely in our seats. They evoke something like political participation. But they also allow the majority of those present to do absolutely nothing.

The presenter is invited to describe where they live. *Blank* gives the actor a lot of opportunities for self-deprecating audience ingratiation, as they are asked to give their weight, height, and so on forward. "Haha! I'm starting to like this," the actor is told to say. "If you'd like to pay me a visit, I live at . . .": Mel revealed that she lived not far away from the theatre (4). She went on, invited by the script, to describe the furnishings of her house: her husband had redecorated their bedroom pink, for example, which she didn't really like. The script inveigles itself into the householding culture of the cities in which it is performed. Celebrity performers are likely to live in aspirational spaces. The pseudo-democratic process continued: "Let's have a vote again," Mel asked, following the script, "Would you mind raising your hand if you feel you know me now?" (5). All of this brought out our quiescent tendencies as an audience. Most of us raised our hands, nudging us forward as the script intended. The script's consensus reality—the performance space to which we all formally assented—was set to the level of a celebrity's home. We were drawn into self-recognition as an audience around its furnishings.

As *Blank* moves through its series of exercises inviting performer and audience to fill in its blanks, it invokes an imprecise repressive political context, as in a game called "Shoot my Past" (6). The script instructs the actor to invite an audience member to act as a "sniper," shouting words at the actor as an attempt to jar a response out of them. Soleimanpour's plays all involve these sudden, unsettling tonal shifts. This one felt unearned: the play provided no details of life either in Iran or in the UK that might warrant such an outlandish comparison between being shot and potentially revealing a truth. "Shoot my Past" didn't jar Mel, who continued to be her ebullient self. As the script explains, the participant is given three words, and

> Each bullet is a word: a simple word that YOU will pick. Words like *Mum, Elephants*, or *Michael Jackson*. / Words like *Michael Jackson* will not hit my heart, at least not as deep as the word *MUM*. You can also aim at my head; ask me a maths question, or throw me a philosophical phrase about life.
>
> (7)

Here again, the script's purpose was less to state anything of particular interest in its own right than to stir the ideas present in the room, seeing what was brought to the surface. "And how can you see how deep you have hit me?," the actor asks: "By hearing my moans!" (7).

Of the three words that our sniper brought up, only "God!" scored any memorable effect on Mel. Raised Catholic although by her own admission lapsed, Mel predicted she would be running back towards the Church as death approached. The script's invocation of universal concerns produced this particular local inflection, the reaction of the member of a largely secular mainstream culture to universal human concerns about mortality. Mel's take on things further emphasised the freedom of choice that our society takes as one of its defining features: religion was something that she could return to as she wished.

The script shifts to invite the sustained participation of one audience member. Mel continued:

> Each one of you could be the main character of a good story about life. All of you ARE the main character in the story of your own life. / Ladies and Gentlemen, / Is there anyone among you who is willing to become our Character?
> (18)

Our volunteer was a tall, statuesque woman named Heather, in blue jeans and a fitted black top. We found out from questions that she was 29 and an actress. The script solicited what it calls the Character—Heather—to answer quickly, writing down her responses on sheets of paper. It did not give her any opportunity to reflect or reframe what she was saying. "In the last few years I have been busy with . . ." acting (54). "I worked in . . ." an office (55). The audience laughed at this: the difficulty of being a young actor is proverbial. "LAST YEAR: The most important thing that happened to me was." Heather paused for a self-assertive half-second. "I had a threesome," she announced, followed by a quieter "it changed my life" (57).

English pandemonium: polite, quiet, nevertheless intense. Mel looked faintly overloaded. She had been up to this moment the most noticeable person onstage. Heather's threesome quietly tore this apart. The performance stopped; for a while, the blandly affirmative generalisations of a certain kind of international theatre was forgotten.

The details. It turned out that she had been making a paralympics-related commercial for Malteasers, a parodically commonplace English semi-savoury sweet, and one thing had sort of led to the other. It happened "organically," she explained, a few days after the shoot. My own notes sort of give out here. I don't remember what Heather had for breakfast, or how she got to the theatre, both items prompted by the script. I do, however, recall Heather's recollection of the moments before appearing onstage: "When I was picked to be this person I thought" "shit" (73). "RIGHT NOW, AT THIS VERY MOMENT, I AM FEELING" "unburdened" (75). Again, the audience went wild.

The town hall-like charisma battle between performer and Heather, our audience delegate, nevertheless held itself apart from the neighbourhood in which it was performed. Mel read out to Heather, "Dear Character, / In this story, we don't care if you have a car or good friends who can drive you home. Tonight, you'll be going home by cab" (89). This nameless, summonable cab driver was like the Deliveroo drivers in *Yerma* (chapter 6), a reliable presence that we can summon at will without caring too much about. As Mel read out, Heather was instructed to fill in the blanks of what her cab driver would look like: "So the cab driver will pick you up at the entrance. He has . . . hair, / Wears a silver. . . ., / And looks . . ." (92–4). It's assumed that the cab driver will be a man, and more overtly religious than normal. This is of course what Uber and other cab-replacement software allow us to do: check up on the looks of our drivers, give us a chance to see if we like them or not. *Blank* frames those of us in the audience as the cab-taking classes; we're interested in the people who drive us around, but only up to a point.

The script also frames us as in control of the story of our lives—but also, unreliant on state assistance. Its final phase asked the Character to speculate on the remainder of her life, through questions such as "I will spend the last ten years of my life in . . ." (162). Heather's plan involved living collectively with a group of "mates" in a disused horse farm in the countryside. She did not imagine any state assistance in this later life scenario. Her solution was privatised: something that she and her friends would undertake on her own. This is how ownership as a paradigm resonates through society: not simply in the day-to-day facts of who lives where and how this is paid for, but even in our imagination of our future. That Heather was not a playwright deliberately trying to reflect on society, but rather an audience member brought onstage to react to a script, made her reaction all the more telling of the hold this mindset has on our moment.

The script invited the Character to reflect further on the end of her life. "The last five years of my life will be even more different. / I will be suffering from . . ." "dementia" (169). Heather's response could not have addressed a more of-the-moment concern; nor, sadly, could it have more thoroughly reflected the dominant ethos of contemporary privatisation. The daily visual culture of London, indeed of the UK more generally, is dominated by advertisements for dementia: dementia awareness, running against dementia, Dementia Awareness Week, an annual Care & Dementia Show—a trade fair—complementing the Alzheimer's Show. All of these shows propose private solutions to the perceived inadequacy of later-life care under the NHS. We fear it even more than death: the inability to make choices; the dependence on others. And, in this privatised social service environment, we fear being farmed (this the term used) out to an unscrupulous private operator, our humanity grievously reduced in the name of corporate efficiency. Heather's mate-stocked horse farm was an attempt to ward this off—to imagine an alternative to a state sector that did not seem able, from our present-day vantage point, to care for us in our old age.

Heather's responses framed her, relentlessly, as an individual. Guided by the script, she set out a plan for herself that did not draw on any kind of shared resources. These responses presented another version of what I have termed *exhausted radicalism and the hedonistic body*: its defining moment was a sex act, around which the rights won by earlier political drives for collective rights appeared haphazardly if at all. The performance instead reflected our current political moment's emphasis consumer choice. The play invites us, via our onstage surrogate, to choose a path through the remainder of our lives, implying we would be in control of them. It then implies that we will furnish these outcomes for ourselves.

2 *White Rabbit, Red Rabbit* (16 September 2017)

A red rabbit, as Soleimanpour fashions it, is someone who risks everything to make it onto a stage. A theatre is a free country, where their voice can be heard. One influential discourse around London itself maintains that is a place for strivers and risk-takers. As mayor, Boris Johnson, in promoting new buses for London, promoted a feature (since disabled) that allowed riders to get on and off between stops, like older London buses did:

> This bus stands for freedom, and choice. . . . It restores to the streets of London the open platform at the rear—and in so doing, it restores the concept of a reasonable risk . . . if the bus got stuck in traffic, or at the lights, you knew that you weren't a prisoner. You were allowed to get on and off at will, provided the thing wasn't moving, and now that freedom and benefit will be restored. . . . It is, as far as I know, one of the few recent examples of a public policy that actually gives back, to sentient and responsible adults, the chance to take an extra risk in return for a specific reward.[11]

Solemainpour could not have known it when he was writing his play, but this is precisely the sort of rhetoric that it appeals to. The quintessential state of being in London, as Johnson describes it—and as *WRRR* flatters it—is of not being imprisoned; of being able to calculate at a moment's one chances and take risks.

Recent immigration policy has encouraged only migration by those who do not require state support. The new migrant is equally affective special case and entrepreneur—red rabbit and negotiator—able to convince an extant society to give them a chance. *WRRR* flatters its audiences that we, too, are special cases: a secret community drawn forth from the general mob. We could be tough and resilient together: it would be our community versus the world. We could take care of ourselves—like Heather planned to, in her old age.

For an evening, *WRRR* let us think about the dangers of public expression in a theatrical environment of absolute safety. The red rabbit, like the Character in *Blank*, is framed as having made it to the stage through individual talent. The evening's performance was a testament to what he could do, collectively, with us: he might even lead to a celebrity being killed. But there was no actual vulnerability in the space that was created. *WRRR*, particularly with the playwright in the building, gave the form of a danger we could not reasonably have expected to exist. It used the dynamics of liveness to make us reflect on lives that in the context of a licensed London performance could only be safe and regulated. We knew the state had our backs. In terms proposed by Lauren Berlant, *WRRR* offered a "redemptive story" that proposes we, like the red rabbit, inhabit a "secure space liberated from identity and structures that seem to constrain what a person can do in history": that London was a place of unrestricted freedoms flying in the face of an obtrusive state elsewhere.[12] It brought the migrant story down to the level of a talented individual whose skill is his proof of concept.

Soleimanpour's plays, as we have seen, create a particular sort of structured conversation. Everyone in the theatre is given at least some chance to speak: so, at the beginning of the piece, we all read out what number audience member we were. *WRRR* invites an engaged, participating audience—but often does so to show how compliant everyone is with requests made by the performer. Soleimanpour has claimed that this, and not conditions in Iran, is the real topic of the piece: "I'm sorry and sick of hearing that I'm writing about my country. I'm writing about a social phenomenon, which is obedience."[13]

For all that it addresses the downsides of authoritarian strictures, *WRRR* has a strongly coercive element to it. The instructions to the performer, for example, tells them they must follow the script exactly: "You may make a mistake in your reading. That's fine. But I need you to go back, and correct it" (np). In turn, the performance, in which a trained and usually well-known actor elicits responses from audience members, corrals and controls these responses. This celebrity association, however, promotes an uneven onstage power dynamic between the performer and those brought up onstage, potentially giving the latter a sort of deer-in-headlights quality.

Our performer for the night was Meera Syal, CBE: a television performer, novelist, and essayist. Relative to the other performers I saw, Syal inflected her performance the least: she read the material faithfully, keeping the performance to the time allotted to it. Unlike *Blank*, the script did not really provide many opportunities for Syal to address herself. Syal opened by announcing the play's structuring conceit: that the evening's celebrity may or may not die at its conclusion through the collusion of the theatre and the script:

> From now on we are ALL present. And NOW I put my vial of deadly poison next to the two glasses of water which are on stage! / Yes, my dear actor, that WAS an instruction! The vial you were given when you got here should not be positioned beside the two water glasses. Well done.
>
> (2)

Syal placed all of these onstage, where they would remain until at the conclusion, she drank from one of them, and lay down, potentially poisoned. We had all been warned not to google the play. I will confess that I read it before the performance, and so lost some of the ostensibly earth-shattering shock of what happens.

And yet: being in the presence of a performance does strange things. I found myself going through phases of credulity and disbelief. It seemed pretty clear the Bush Theatre was not going to murder the performer on a stage. The play made everyone present reflect on the society that was putting on the play: those who directed and stage managed the production; those who run the theatre, and those who licence it, and ultimately to the system of laws that would punish whoever actually slipped the performer poison. There was the added wrinkle of social media: word would have gotten out if celebrities were actually being murdered as part of a semi-obscure theatrical death ritual. I wondered, idly, if there were places where the impossibility of onstage death might not be the case, perhaps in politically coercive parts of the world. Would it have been different to see this in a tiny venue, perhaps a bit uncertain about who the performer was, before the play was better known?

Serving as the playwright's mouthpiece and framed onstage by his ostensible murder machine, Syral proceeded through a script that was broadly consistent with the contemporary English ethos of consumer choice. Like *Blank*, *WRRR* is characterised by wild shifts in mode and manner. It begins earnestly, with Soleimanpour introducing himself: "I was born on Azar 19th, 1360 in Tehran. That's December 10th, 1981 in Christian years. I'm Iranian, and being Iranian neither offends nor satisfies me" (19). The script reaches out to a global audience at a moment when the rhetoric of consumer culture has taken hold across a broad swathe of national political cultures.[14] He addresses the audience as fellow individuals making a judgement about whether their nationality "satisfies" them or not. We're addressed as people who, like the playwright, have the ability to think outside of our immediate surroundings, to consider national situations beyond our own—but our transnationalism is consumer transnationalism, even of our own citizenship.

The audience is addressed as having more freedom than the voice of the script, the playwright unable to travel:

> You see, it tastes like FREEDOM to know there are these OTHER people in one's play and it tastes like FREEDOM to be able to travel to OTHER worlds through my words. . . . Oh my dear god! Would you save a seat for me? An empty seat for me in the front row?!
>
> (21)

The power of the audience so exceeds that of the playwright that he is a virtual non-presence, powerless to stop them. The performer describes him as in danger: "Sometimes I get scared writing this play. I feel I'm designing a BIG GUN which will shoot somebody one day. Maybe even myself" (35). We free audience members were observing the playwright, discursively, taking a risk—refusing to simply exist in a place that did not satisfy him.

Imogen Tyler notes the way the contemporary politics of migration sort minority groups—both new migrants, and those descended from them—into successes and failures.[15] Soleimanpour conforms to many aspects of the migrant who gets through: flattering local customs, self-deprecating of his "terrorist" self in front of the sorts of audiences who might pat themselves on the back for not sharing this common prejudice against Iranians (I do a good line in Canadian self-apology, myself; I recognised the endearment strategy.) He even invites us to write to him directly: "That's 'nassim,' spelled N.A.S.S.I.M. dot S.N at gmail dot com" (23). He notes in fact that "Facebook is filtered in Iran"—he asks us instead to write to him through Google, which has played nicer with the Iranian authorities.

This is a play about strivers: those whose lives don't satisfy them, who hustle, who game a difficult system, and who feel (in this framing) the greatest burden of state interference. "White Rabbit Red Rabbit," the script explains, refers to an alleged experiment in animal husbandry. Before his uncle killed himself, the play claims, Soleimanpour's uncle used to perform experiments on rabbits. They would be encouraged to run up a ladder and eat a carrot; the one who got there first, and got the carrot, he painted red. He then doused the white rabbits with cold water. Afterwards, the red rabbit would be attacked by the other rabbits; he would be removed from the cage, and the experiment repeated again. Even after removing the ice water bath, the same thing happens: the red rabbits would always be attacked. There's no way of verifying if these experiments were ever run: if this is a universal truth about rabbit sociology. This is more like a fable: a story with a hidden message, which the audience is invited to interpret.

An audience member invited onstage to be the "red rabbit." I cannot speak to what this play might be like in societies where performances are closely monitored or banned: where the play's moderately elliptical nature might point to provocative truths or contradictions in local society. The performances noted on the website—the ones with celebrity performers—have been for the most part in New York, Los Angeles, and London: cities that tend not to imprison playwrights. And in these cities, which can present to the limited demographic that makes up theatre audiences a strong sense of itself, the vagueness of what *WRRR* can leave it feeling pretty much like an emptily affirmative ritual. The piece asked the audience to collude with the white rabbit, but only in terms of following the rules:

> Oh, / I totally / forgot to / explain this. / Rabbits are to cover their ears / when they go to the circus. / You know why, of course? / Because if they DON'T, the audience sitting / BEHIND them will not be able to SEE. . . . It's the rule of the circus.

(10)

The Circus is a place of arbitrary rules concerning the freedom of performance: rules quite different from those of performances in London. So, the performance stops while a hat is asked for the rabbit. On this evening, the audience found such a hat—presumably, the theatre had one to spare in case they didn't. They made him one of their own. But in doing so, they also upheld the rules of the circus, adapting them to this local environment. We are brought into fellowship with the rabbit—and, in particular, with his just getting by in the world of the circus.

When he wrote the play, Soleimanpour could not travel; in the various figures of oppression—bears, crows—he created figures that on some level stood in for political oppression, revealing his plight wherever his plays were performed. He has the performer yell at the volunteer red rabbit: "As for the red rabbit—YOU PRICK. YOU PIECE OF SHIT. You think you're so fucking smart? Should I get them to beat you? Do you want this one to rip your FUCKING GUTS OUT?! FUCK YOU!!" (41). The performer, Soleimanpour's mouthpiece, mimed being the white rabbits—the less ambitious multitude—on the behalf of the audience. A London theatre blogger who writes as "Billi" found moments such as this challenging: "I've never been to the theatre," she writes, "and been made to feel inadequate as an audience member before."[16] Yet the script ventriloquised our white rabbit blood lust in a way that felt slightly hyperbolic. None of us were this irritated with the red rabbit—we were mostly probably relieved, that someone else was taking on the burden of audience participation. We were not really white rabbits, given how unsubtly they were portrayed. We were not braying for the blood of those on stage. So, we could tell ourselves, we were ourselves red rabbits, or at least their enablers: those who would allow the performance to continue.

The stage becomes the liberatory space where for a moment the rabbit can elude the bears and stand before the audience. As the story progresses,

> The bears try to drag the rabbit out. The rabbit resists, but how much CAN a rabbit resist? How many bears can a red rabbit take on? A bear stumbles. The rabbit escapes. S/he leaps away. The bears chase her/him. In a flash, the rabbit reaches the STAGE.
>
> (14)

In its original performances, when Soleimanpour was still confined to Iran, the audience member—playing the rabbit—became his incarnation upon the stage. Now, though, with Soleimanpour in the theatre with us, the performance became a sort of victory lap for his apparent escape from Iran and arrival in London.

The talk of red and white rabbits—of driven achievers and vengeful sluggards holding them back—flattered a room full of Londoners. "What are the limits of OBEDIENCE?," the Actor asked us, "How often will CONFORMITY control your thoughts, my rabbits?" (25). Red rabbit-hood is part of London's self-description, and the voice of the play addressed us as such: "The IMPORTANT fact is that you've succeeded in separating yourself from the others and climbing the steps of the carrot ladder to reach my text" (58). We had done exactly what the red rabbit had done: taken a risk, received a specific reward. Although at the conclusion we saw Syal drink the glass of ostensible poison, we knew that the "murder machine" wasn't real. Despite the play's protestations towards its conclusion—"What if number 5 really poisoned her/his glass? . . . What if the produces are DICKHEADS and used REAL poison?"—we ascertained we were in the good place, the place where the script's voice had projected itself into (53). We had helped, collectively, the play's voice realise its ambitions.

As it happens, Shepherd's Bush is one of the nearest Underground stations to Grenfell Tower, site only a few months previously of the largest social housing disaster in English history, in one of the wealthiest boroughs in England. Seventy-one residents of a nearby housing estate were killed by a multiple failure of regulation and planning: "The tower, which had a hundred and twenty-nine apartments, had been refurbished the previous year and covered with a form of aluminium cladding that is banned in the U.S. and elsewhere in Europe as a fire risk."[17] The cladding had been chosen specifically for the cost savings it presented. These austerity governments will not be talked subsequently about without mention of Grenfell. The event encapsulates what happens when everything public is done, as cheaply as possible, with market incentives in mind.

Residents on the top floor of the Grenfell building were instructed to remain in their apartments, where many of them died. These instructions were, in other words, precisely what Soleimanpour invokes: a "suicide machine," a seemingly counterintuitive set of instructions that tested their recipients' faith in social systems. The instructions were not, precisely, wrong—for correctly administrated buildings. The National Fire Chiefs Council, for example, notes that these instructions are "based on effective fire safety arrangements that are required, proposed, and then provided in the building."[18] The instructions provide a best-case plan for surviving a fire, providing that support systems are in place. Some in the tower understood this, and followed these instructions.[19] *WRRR*, several months later, presented its audience with a similar proposition: have faith in the social organism. A similar faith underwrites the "risk" Johnson proposed in his new London buses: London traffic is not anarchy, but rather a carefully ordered system, held in place by regulations. What these vastly different outcomes revealed, however, was a fragmented plethora of risk degrees within the experience of those living in the city. If we had thought the "death machine" of *WRRR* posed a thousandth of a threat of faulty building cladding, we audience members would mostly certainly have cleared it from the stage—but we ascertained, correctly, that what happened in a London theatre was too regulated to allow this to occur. In a performance that flattered the space that permitted it to be put on, the play created a sense among audience members of a safety that they enjoyed unevenly.

Although they were not written specifically for London, Soleimanpour's plays responds well to the city's embrace of the striver. It acknowledges universal rights, while also suggesting that some rabbits are more equal than others: "Of course, it is always, and sometimes only, the red rabbit who pays the highest price" (56). A lot of cities tell this story about themselves, and theatres are overwhelmingly most likely to be in cities. This audience could leave the theatre feeling good that England is not a repressive state that would hold such strivers back. Yet these plays do not stage anything like open discussion or dissent. There's no contingency written into the plays for, say, what would happen if an audience member ran up on stage and spirited the poison away. All of us present relied on the essentially predictable nature of performance at a licenced venue in a country where performance is permitted. We relied on the society that failed at Grenfell.

By encouraging its audience volunteers to answer quickly, and placing them under the constant control of the Actor, *Blank* created a sort of echo chamber for the concerns of those capable of making it to the theatre. These pieces reward their audiences for making it out to the theatre, figured as a place of freedom; they even put audience members onstage to receive freedom's rewards. A story of motivated red rabbits escaping from a field of violent white ones rewards those who have already made it; it forecloses a space to think about those who have not. I cannot speak to the uses Soleimanpour's work might be put to in other contexts—in places where their conundrums about freedom might seem more provocative than staid, more battles yet to be won than those established in the past, at least for the theatre-attending classes. Yet at the Bush Theatre, Soleimanpour's plays created yet another machine for letting comfortable people (like Mel, of the pink bedroom interiors) feel their state of privileged exception was one of universal belonging. Only Heather's Millennial self-assertion was able to cut through the self-reinforcing normality. Yet her contribution lives on only in a couple of Tweets about Malteasers attached to the show.[20] *Blank* gave Heather a one-off victory—as it might to any participant in the role of Character—but at end of the evening, Mel was still the celebrity. *WRRR* asked us to take part in an already-completed drama of ingratiating migration: the red rabbit had gotten through, and the playwright was in the theatre with us. Yet *Blank's* offhand reference to the cab driver shows a lesser regard for wider populations—a lack of regard that, in light of Grenfell, should give us pause. *WRRR* encourages us to accommodate ourselves to the rules of the Circus—to find a hat for the rabbit, to make whatever sort of accommodation we can to allow him to get through.

Our participation had rewarded Soleimanpour's entrepreneurship. He was the sort of immigrant the city welcomes—indeed, that any city would welcome. His scripts reward the entrepreneur's simultaneous disruptive personal initiative and limited desire to make structural stage: the daring red rabbit, racing to the stage while making no change to the operation of the Circus. As in many stories that emphasise the dynamic and the deserving, our empathetic capacity is taken up with the ingratiating individual who fulfils the categories that we already recognise as our own. This held doubly or even trebly true in these performances, with the actual playwright on hand with a cohort of celebrity performers backing him up. Nothing succeeds like success.

This festival would need to have been scheduled long before the events of 2017 occurred. No one involved in the Bush Theatre's festival, much less the playwright himself, was in any sense culpable for the events of Grenfell—events too terrible, and too raw, for me to write about without some sense that I am invoking them too lightly. I've called Soleimanpour flattering and entrepreneurial—but I've been both, myself, to arrive here, and with greater advantages of nationality (at least in terms of national circulability), to boot. We're all of us caught up inside so many negative things, most beyond any theatre's ability to redress: the lack of non-white (much less non-Western) writers appearing in London theatres, the difficulty of playwrights from authoritarian countries finding voice in any context, the difficulty of young actors to find work. Even the beneficence of established actors willing to take a punt on a weird one-off appears in these pages more negatively than I mean it to. We were all trying our best; the scale of the tragedy mocked our efforts. These two remarkable, memorable evenings of performance showed how readily well-meaning people could come together to agree to a consensus reality whose pattern of risk and reward was true mostly for ourselves. So many wanted a place in London. Some died for it, for no reason beyond the meanest sort of political expediency. There'd been a "machine for ending life" all along—these plays had made it feel as though it wasn't for us, those wandering back into the West London night (55).

Notes

1 "Croydon vs. the World," *Croydon vs. the World*, undated. https://croydonvstheworld. teemill.co.uk/.
2 Tim Butler, "Living in the Bubble: Gentrification and Its 'Others' in North London," *Urban Studies* 40, no. 12 (2003): 2470.
3 The visa had previously required individuals to hold £100,000 within the country; this was reduced to £50,000. In May 2019, the visa category was replaced with a "UK Innovator" visa requiring the same amount of funds to be shown but a more complex endorsement process.
4 Mark Rice-Oxley, "Grenfell: The 72 Victims, Their Lives, Loves and Losses," *The Guardian* (London), May 14, 2018, www.theguardian.com/uk-news/2018/may/14/grenfell-the-71-victims-their-lives-loves-and-losses.
5 Ibid.
6 For the most recent projections as they were at this writing (25 June 2020), see Michael Savage, "More Than Half of England's Coronavirus-Related Deaths Will Be People from Care Homes," *The Observer* (London), June 7, 2020, www.theguardian. com/society/2020/jun/07/more-than-half-of-englands-coronavirus-related-deaths-will-be-people-from-care-homes. BAME citizens also appear to be disproportionately impacted, although precise numbers and an overarching cause are at present unclear.
7 *The Jungle* (Young Vic 2017), which subsequently received a West End transfer, made an immersive experience out of the migrant camps at the entrance to the Channel Tunnel; it ends with the camp being broken up by police, and a single actor making it through to England in effect to convene the play. The Bush Theatre itself staged Estelle Savasta's *Going Through* (2018), about a solo female migrant to England who makes a successful asylum bid and joins the NHS, the next year.
8 All citations are to the editions of the plays found in Nassim Soleimanpour, *Two Plays* (London: Oberon Books, 2017). They are provided with page numbers, and cited inline, when page numbers are available; however, not all of the book is consistently paginated.
9 Qtd. in Kelsey Jacobson, "(Dis)Embodied Authority in *White Rabbit, Red Rabbit*," *Canadian Theatre Review* 158 (2014): 78.
10 Thom Dibdin, "*Nassim* Review at Traverse Theatre, Edinburgh," *The Stage*, 2017, www.thestage.co.uk/reviews/2017/nassim-review-traverse-theatre-edinburgh-emotionally-charged-theatrical-experiment/.
11 Dave Hill, "Boris's Bus (A Political Journey) Part 43: No More 'Hop On, Hop Off'?" *The Guardian* (London), June 23, 2015, Boris's Bus (A Political Journey) Part 43: No More 'Hop On, Hop Off'?

12 Lauren Berlant, *The Queen of America Goes to Washington City* (Durham, NC: Duke University Press, 1997), 21.

13 "Playwright Nassim Soleimanpour Sees His Own Play," *BBC News*, 2013, www.bbc.co.uk/news/entertainment-arts-21577030.

14 See, for example, David Harvey, *A Brief History of Neoliberalism* (Oxford: Oxford University Press, 2005), 41 and passim.

15 Imogen Tyler, *Revolting Subjects: Social Abjection and Resistance in Neoliberal Britain* (London: Zed Books Ltd., 2013).

16 "Billi, 'Theatre Review: White Rabbit Red Rabbit'," *The View from the Circle*, *Blogspot* (blog), September 13, 2017, http://viewfromthecircle.blogspot.co.uk/2017/09/theatre-review-white-rabbit-red-rabbit.html.

17 Sam Knight, "The Year the Grenfell Tower Fire Revealed the Lie That Londoners Tell Themselves," *The New Yorker*, December 27, 2017, www.newyorker.com/culture/2017-in-review/the-year-the-grenfell-tower-fire-revealed-the-lie-that-londoners-tell-themselves.

18 "Stay Put Position Statement," *National Fire Chiefs Council*, www.nationalfirechiefs.org.uk/Stay-Put-position.

19 The Equality and Human Rights Commission (EHRC) report on the disaster notes multiple dimensions of failings. The " 'stay put' policy was devised as an alternative to evacuation in buildings designed and constructed to contain a fire," as Grenfell's altered cladding meant it no longer was (6). Access to how the policy was to work was distributed unevenly and without adequate opportunities for questions to be asked: "Information provided to residents about fire risk and safety measures were variable at best, and residents had no effective way of raising concerns" (6). Finally, the information that was presented was given in such a way that it was hard to access for "children, pregnant women, older people, disabled people and those not fluent in English" (7). (*Summary of Submissions Following Phase 1 of the Grenfell Tower Inquiry* [London: Employment and Human Rights Commission, 2019]. https://www.nationalfirechiefs.org.uk/Stay-Put-position.)

20 See, for example, a tweet from an actor who was in attendance for the performance: "Nassim Soleimanpour's 'BLANK' @bushtheatre with #MelGiedroyc tonight was just hysterical & wonderful & so much fun. . .#maltesers." (Sophie Ablett, [@sophie__ablett], September 11, 2017, 10:53 pm, https://twitter.com/sophieablett/status/907361601833127937).

Works cited

Berlant, Lauren. *The Queen of America Goes to Washington City*. Durham, NC: Duke University Press, 1997.

"Billi, 'Theatre Review: White Rabbit Red Rabbit'." *The View from the Circle*. *Blogspot*, September 13, 2017. http://viewfromthecircle.blogspot.co.uk/2017/09/theatre-review-white-rabbit-red-rabbit.html.

Butler, Tim. "Living in the Bubble: Gentrification and Its 'Others' in North London." *Urban Studies* 40, no. 12 (2003): 2469–86.

"Croydon vs. the World." *Croydon vs. the World*. Undated. https://croydonvstheworld.tee-mill.co.uk/.

Dibdin, Thom. "*Nassim* Review at Traverse Theatre, Edinburgh." *The Stage*, August 6, 2017. www.thestage.co.uk/reviews/2017/nassim-review-traverse-theatre-edinburgh-emotionally-charged-theatrical-experiment/.

Harvey, David. *A Brief History of Neoliberalism*. Oxford: Oxford University Press, 2005.

Hill, Dave. "Boris's Bus (a Political Journey) Part 43: No More 'Hop on, Hop Off'?" *The Guardian* (London), June 23, 2015. Boris's Bus (A Political Journey) Part 43: No More 'Hop On, Hop Off'?

Jacobson, Kelsey. "(Dis)Embodied Authority in *White Rabbit, Red Rabbit.*" *Canadian Theatre Review* 158 (2014): 76–80.

Knight, Sam. "The Year the Grenfell Tower Fire Revealed the Lie That Londoners Tell Themselves." *The New Yorker*, December 27, 2017. www.newyorker.com/culture/2017-in-review/the-year-the-grenfell-tower-fire-revealed-the-lie-that-londoners-tell-themselves

Rice-Oxley, Mark. "Grenfell: The 72 Victims, Their Lives, Loves and Losses." *The Guardian* (London), May 14, 2018. www.theguardian.com/uk-news/2018/may/14/grenfell-the-71-victims-their-lives-loves-and-losses.

Savage, Michael. "More Than Half of England's Coronavirus-Related Deaths Will Be People from Care Homes." *The Observer* (London), June 7, 2020. www.theguardian.com/society/2020/jun/07/more-than-half-of-englands-coronavirus-related-deaths-will-be-people-from-care-homes.

Soleimanpour, Nassim. *Two Plays*. London: Oberon Books, 2017.

Sophie Ablett (@sophie__ablett), September 11, 2017, 10:53 pm. https://twitter.com/sophieablett/status/907361601833127937.

"Stay Put Position Statement." *National Fire Chiefs Council*. Undated. www.nationalfirechiefs.org.uk/Stay-Put-position.

Summary of Submissions Following Phase 1 of the Grenfell Tower Inquiry. London: Equality and Human Rights Commission, 2019. https://www.equalityhumanrights.com/sites/default/files/summary-of-submissions-following-phase1-of-the-grenfell-tower-inquiry.pdf.

Tyler, Imogen. *Revolting Subjects: Social Abjection and Resistance in Neoliberal Britain*. London: Zed Books Ltd., 2013.

Youngs, Ian. "Playwright Nassim Soleimanpour Sees His Own Play." *BBC News*, February 26, 2013. www.bbc.co.uk/news/entertainment-arts-21577030.

6 *Yerma* on the internet

Yerma (2017) by Simon Stone, adapt. Federico García Lorca
Young Vic Theatre, 66 The Cut, Lambeth, London SE1 8LZ; simulcast to
  ArtHouse Crouch End Cinema, 159A Tottenham Ln, London, N8 9BT
31 August 2017

In many London performances in 2017, property-owning characters and their
concerns pushed all other considerations from the stage. Often, they came right
out and announced this. Consider the following: John, a white man, and his wife,
a white woman, have just bought the London house that should cement stay in the
home-owning classes. In their professional lives they are, by their own description, "two smart, open-minded, liberal, caring individuals, with an awareness of
our duty to the less fortunate."[1] Yet in this home they have purchased, with the
fourth wall dissolved, they reveal their commitment to liberalism is merely formal
and expedient, something they do to get ahead at work:

John: Any given suburb. First there's average working class. Then there's crack
    dealers. Then there's artists come buying from the crack dealers. Then
    they tell their gay friends about the wicked ass neighbourhood they've
    been buying their crack at and the gays are all fuck yeah I can't afford
    Dalston anymore anyhow but the male gays they're too pussy, don't want
    to get their Prada all messed up, but the chicks, they got something to
    prove, they're hard ass lesbian bitches, they come buy a two up two down,
    roll their sleeves up, get their hands dirty and . . .
Her: Lay the first stone of gentrification.

                                                                    (7–8)

Let's call these post-progressive characters. John and his wife, called "Her" in
the script, know they are taking advantage of the social categorisation their liberalism has made them hip to. They are aware of the social problems they have
contributed to, using politically incorrect terms for what they describe. They are
aware that their position is problematic. They acknowledge the forms of social
progress that are available, only to ignore them. Indeed, if they had described

themselves as political conservatives, nothing substantial would have changed about the play.

Was there something similarly post-progressive about the fact of this performance itself? These words were first uttered in the midst of a housing crisis—at a theatre that, as Kim Solga and Joanne Tompkins write, is known for its "firm commitment to its immediate demographic area," the hyper-gentrifying Borough of Lambeth.[2] What is the joke here? Who is it "on"? And who is it for—what community does it build? There is, of course, something like hedonism expressed here: that tired white homeowners can ignore social constraints and finally unload their self-interest and bile. You probably have an easier time sharing in this hedonism if you're not one of the people displaced by gentrification, or called out for the stereotypical aspects of your sexuality. The lack of onstage pushback to these jokes is what I have called *mimetic irony:* humour that reinforces, rather than challenges, the social order as it is. Gays like Prada, lesbians are butches, and the working classes get moved about by the whims of the propertied. We can only speculate whether any given working class or lesbian audience member might find this funny. But the play in which this scene appears, 2016's Young Vic adaptation of *Yerma* by the playwright Simon Stone, also puts no such person—whether lesbian or working class or otherwise—onstage to force such a juxtaposition.

Yerma was also simulcast around the world, as part of the NT Live program: a further displacement of the local conditions in which it was performed. *Yerma* is approximately tragic: its main character kills herself. These homeowning characters suffer for their choices—yet are given a totally blank space in which to make them. Their drives and motivations may be self-destructive, but this play takes them very seriously, particularly in staging choices that amplify rather than undercut them: strobe lights to convey their anxieties, actors doubled in roles to reflect their delusions. Writing about another fertility drama, Victoria Sadler notes that "[w]hen global issues and stories are explored, we have to move away from the White woman being at the centre of the story."[3] These staging choices do the opposite, pushing this white woman not just towards the centre of the story but even towards our ability to focus on it. The shock to her system registers in our own; we couldn't see other presences, even if they had been onstage.

Adapted from a heavily abstract 1930s drama by the Spanish playwright Frederico García Lorca, this *Yerma* collapses the early play's mythical resonances and potentials into an account of the inevitability of society remaining the way it is. Considered abstractly from the drama of its main characters, it shows a London neighbourhood moving from a historical place with particular communities and contextual resonances into an abstract domestic void. In what follows I read *Yerma's* staging—particularly its use of strobe effects, sharp scene changes, and intertitles—as shocking the audience into emotional identification with debt-driven lifestyle choices. Occupying the queer space of Lorca's *Yerma* means that other stories, particularly those of the poor, can't live there—exactly the sort of displacement the characters John and his wife joke about. Stone's *Yerma* tells a local story shows privileged characters wrestling with the expanded opportunities offered to the privileged—and, moreover, shows them doing so outside of any local community. Denying the distance of Lorca's play from its original setting, this new staging dismantled the tools we might use to dig ourselves out of our present moment—particularly, its normalisation of financial debt.

"Financialisation" describes the coming to prominence of the financial services industries within a national economy. *Yerma* reflects this. The play's central couple uses a mortgage to, by their own description, displace the previous occupants of their neighbourhood. They next pursue in vitro fertilization (IVF) treatments, funded by consumer debt, in their finally unsuccessful attempts to conceive a child. *Yerma* frames this as a tragedy with no externalities. No one outside of the household is harmed by this couple's actions. The staging puts no critical presence in the way of debt—in fact detonates, while we watch, tools for critical thinking. It offers us no local resistance to it: no character who speaks out against it, nor the critical tools to imagine a life outside of its continual presence. The play's seeming satirical elements, its knowing in-jokes about London insiders, are ultimately regressive: they stand in the way of critical awareness, rather than promote it.

Founded as an offshoot of the National Theatre, the Young Vic sits in Lambeth, Southwark, down the road from Waterloo Station. Traditionally the Young Vic has been associated with increasing theatrical accessibility for adolescents and young adults. In more recent times, as the theatre became another major London institution, it developed a focus on serious interactions with its surrounding community. That same 2017 season included a particularly fine *Suppliant Women* whose cast was mainly young female actors from the surrounding community. The *Suppliant Women* realised the bodies of Aeschylus' protection-seeking women in people who lived near the theatre, in the process making real the plight of contemporary refugees. *Yerma* was not a community production—but it borrowed some of the realistic force, the whiff of nearbyness, that productions like the *Suppliant Women* built up. The characters in *Yerma* could potentially be residents of the neighbourhood near the theatre. The house that the main female character, simply named Her, and her husband buy could be near the Young Vic, or maybe a bit further out in South London. Tellingly, it was *Yerma*, rather than the *Suppliant Women*, which was simulcast around the world.

Audiences queued up for online tickets to the play's 2017 return. Missing the sale date meant seeing the simulcast. Even in London, the simulcast audience was potentially larger than the Young Vic's: Crouch End, where I watched the broadcast, had no less than two venues showing it. Globally, the audience was larger by several orders of magnitude. Simulcasting takes dramas out of the neighbourhoods in which they are performed. When we walk to the theatre's actual location in Lambeth, we can (for example) observe gentrification in action, observing the contrasts and coherences between new high-rise buildings, post-war council flats, Victorian train station architecture. I don't want to be falsely utopic about live performance: for the majority of audiences, simulcasting is the only way to see *Yerma* or plays like it. I merely want to note that they have a greater potential for creating deracinated, floating experiences—an opportunity that *Yerma* took full advantage of, setting its action in a void that emphasised its affluent main characters' actions over the setting in which those actions took place.

Simulcasting offers opportunities and disadvantages in presenting theatre—but, by all accounts, it fundamentally changes the nature of what it broadcasts. A marked difference is its ability to give audiences close shots of actors' faces, of the sort that would be impossible for anyone sitting in the actual theatre. In general, a stage offers a relatively even field of comparison: everyone appearing on a blank stage has at least some claim to the audience's attention, manipulated by (say) their relative placement upstage or downstage in a proscenium arch stage. In contrast, a simulcast may put its audiences closer to individual actors, at the expense of the overall mise en scene. Alison Stone describes how simulcasting emphasises emotional over more critical sorts of audience awareness, with "market research in 2009 show[ing] NT Live audiences found the broadcasts more emotionally engaging than did audiences who saw the same production live in the theater."[4] *Yerma*'s tight focus on one character does this too. A play about strong egoism is matched with a medium that can bring an audience closer to an individual's experience, as expressed by an actor's face or body. This dynamic, further, multiplies some of the retreats from community built into Stone's script. The bare space of the *Yerma* performance staged a retreat from the play's neighbourhood. The simulcast's occasional focus on actors' faces sustained a further retreat still, away from the stage ensemble and towards an individual character.

Something analogous happened in the play's adaptation, which converted the open-endedness of the original's story into something closer to what a well-off contemporary audience would find familiar. Simulcasts insist on adding extra content, as if to make up for our not being there: special features on the theatre, interviews with the actors, that sort of thing. The *Yerma* broadcast was framed by an interview with the adapter and director, Simon Stone. Stone specialises in what he terms "overwriting": taking a classic drama and improvising a new script for it during rehearsals, resulting in something approximately the same shape as the original but almost entirely changed line for line. When asked what sort of an adaptation this play was, Stone said that this Yerma was from the "same myth" as Lorca's, but otherwise a different piece of theatre.[5]

The original concerns young, newly married peasants in rural Spain, what is termed by the stage directions a "A barren, hot land of children."[6] This description evokes a range of political, religious, and aesthetic possibilities—figurative and literal. It is, as Kimberley Ramírez writes, "a performance text that evokes moods rather than portraying static places or characters," conveying an unease both politically relevant to 1930s Span but also transcending it.[7] In the original, Yerma is 15, her husband slightly older; they, too, cannot conceive a child. Juan has an unspecified sexual problem; both Yerma and Juan are menaced by symbols of one sort or another, from the ghostly Child who keeps appearing at their window to the overtly symbolic events of their lives: "When I first got married and came here, a man carried me over the irrigation channel. It was flooded." The play provides no definitive account for why Yerma is, as her name in Spanish suggests, barren. Her husband Juan seems more interested in sheep, and in sleeping away from Yerma; Dolores, the wise woman of the village, hints at unspecified sexual events in his past. A range of abstract possibilities for barrenness appear—none, in the text at least, confirmed. This is one sense of queerness: political, sexual, or moral possibilities that can find no realisation in the world. The conformity of society is making the characters miserable; they look to the past, or to (for example) whatever the irrigation channel represents, for possible redemption.

Stephens' play is committed to a "mythology" that makes it seem like history's concerns are more or less like our concerns. Lorca wrote a play, with queer overtones, about rural peasant girl: about the overlooked, in other words. Stone's play addresses those with disproportionate cultural influence. This overwriting is a particular problem in the case of Lorca. As his biographer, Ian Gibson, notes, the queer elements of Lorca's biography and canon alike have been ruthlessly suppressed.[8] As Jana Perkovic writes of another Stone production, *Yerma* "is basically a remake, of the kind practiced by Hollywood," in which the potentially difficult, unruly, resistant text . . . has been replaced with its own pliable, submissive clone."[9] Historical texts offer problems that we still perhaps have not solved. The possibility that a text might offer us an imaginative alternative to our present world as it stands is diminished by Stone's approach to adaptation.

As in the Cusk *Medea* I address in my first chapter, Stone's *Yerma* replaces mythological universality with relentless London-specificity—indeed expanding the role of the property-owning in London into a universal caste, those through which the city's experiences are presented. At a telling moment in the play, for example, the main character's mother mentions how excited she is about Internet food delivery. One of the most controversial companies in the UK in the last few years has been Internet food-delivery services hailed for their convenience but accused of paying below-market wages to their employees.[10] The services have, as Izabella Kaminska writes, "permanently changed middle-class urban dweller expectations about how food should be served to them."[11] Piper's character's mother is particularly excited about this: "See all the different options? Isn't that incredible? Takes 20 minutes. And you know exactly how far away the bike, or sometimes it's a scooter, how far away the scooter is. Isn't that incredible?" (34). For characters inside the upper-middle-class bubble that the play depicts, this is a model for interactions with the world: weightless, easily available through the Internet, and totally typical of their times. No Deliveroo driver appears: everyone visible is a salaried professional with a middle-class accent. The staging reproduces, rather than challenges, these characters' worldview.

Over the last few years, London real estate firm Marsh and Parsons has been running real estate ads in the Underground that show the extremes of what I call *resonant ownership*: the way that the only important things within human experience are those that can be privately owned. These ads make exceptionally literal the notion that Londoners are totally subsumed within the property that they own: "A stylishly presented mews house with a beautiful private garden" shows a model-thin, conventionally attractive white woman with a tattooed arm. Piper's character, too, totally commits her body to both biopower and real estate, as when she describes the results of prenatal exercise: "My pelvic floor is like a fucking . . . what's something that's flexible and muscly at the same time? It's like a fucking *octopus*" (61). Like the Marsh and Parsons advertisements, she describes herself as a house. She highlights her expensively maintained pelvic floor, like the three floors of her house, for the approval of others. Real estate imagined as, say, a baby ("New build. Acoustic insulation throughout") has an affective rightness to exist that, say, a former public institution converted into luxury flats does not.

Stone presents a relentless unqueering of Lorca's myth. None of his characters want anything that masses of other people at their income level don't want—indeed, Her tragedy is simply that she wants to have a child past a point that most people would think is reasonable. She is excessively, overwhelmingly normal, down to her insistent desire to have children. IVF treatments were estimated in one much-cited report to have been worth £320 million in 2016 in the UK alone.[12] Can something with this kind of market capitalisation really be called a "myth," as Stone terms it—something that resonates across history, something that has a truth on some level beyond questioning? If it is, this myth flatters a basic, extremely biological understanding of what human beings are like. By implication it reflects a very old understanding of certain gay and trans couples, that their inability to procreate biologically is a sign of some ultimate insufficiency of their existence. Adoption has been common in human history, as have gender and family fluidity. Yet, like many other recent plays about IVF, *Yerma* needed to show the main character's absolute unwillingness to adopt for its plot to function.[13]

Helen: I mean she does know there are millions of orphaned children the world over, doesn't she?
John: Definitely don't say that to her.
Helen: Why not?
John: She doesn't want to. She doesn't want to consider that right now. She still hasn't given up.

(68)

This imagined world of orphans is another kind of normal—another world, with a different set of assumptions of what is important about children.

This is again post-progressive thinking. These are not the sort of people who are unaware of the plight of orphans. They acknowledge that there are bigger problems in the world, but carry on regardless. Because we never find out exactly what it represents, the symbolic Child in Lorca's play might have stood in for outsiders like orphans. Here, we can almost imagine these orphans pressed against the walls of the play's glass set—but definitely not on the stage itself. Among the newspaper reviewers, Michael Billington, writing for the *Guardian*, was a cautious dissenting voice in this regard: "Stone's updated rewrite, however, drastically limits the play. . . . Given the purported radicalism of Piper's character, you also wonder why she subscribes to the notion that child-bearing is the ultimate source of female fulfilment."[14]

Selfishness, within the play, drives sales on the Internet. In a similar way, the play's willingness to show world audiences a readily accessible version of middle-class life drove sales of its Internet simulcast. She is a lifestyle blogger, whose opinions grow more popular the more nakedly selfish her reflections on getting pregnant become. Removing the character's name suggests that there is a universal character to her struggles. But these struggles are so particular to a woman of her time and class that this gesture towards universality foregrounds the play's lack of imaginative connection with those types of people we do not already notice a great deal of via the Internet. All of the characters are at least superficially fluent with the language of gender politics: "Of course yeah deconstruct the thought, explore it, the politics versus the biological impulse" (32). But this language appears as a sort of empty ritual: words mouthed because they're what we expect to hear, rather than something anyone actually believes in. This is what I mean when I call this a post-progressive play: that it shows a society that has developed the intellectual and political tools to achieve progressive social ends, but then abandoned them. These progressive ends are multiple: social housing, gender and racial equality, the acceptance of non-normative sexualities—indeed, of non-normative anything. Within the play, blogging works: she's successful so long as she manages it properly. It's only when her IVF treatments get in the way—when she manages her blogging badly—that she loses her position. The *Yerma* simulcasts in contrast were an expertly managed proposition: beamed around the world, their earnings securing the Young Vic itself.

The play, then, refigures the Lorca "myth" as a story about the management of the body in an age of normalised debt. In Lorca's original, the main character strangles her husband: a different myth, with different resonances. By attacking her husband, Lorca's character attacks what we might think of as the patriarchy: the order of the society that has saddled her with an insufficient husband, dreams, and options. Stone's woman in contrast kills herself over uncertainty. She does not strike at a system larger than her: at the doctors who run the IVF treatments, or even at her husband. Instead, she harms herself.

An upper-middle-class woman in contemporary London does have social options that a poor peasant woman in rural Spain in the 1930s—or indeed the impoverished parts of Lambeth in 2017—does not. Yet this outcome promotes a worldview that elides the differences between them: of health, education, money, just for starters. Taking the play's implicit comparison between the poor and the rich seriously means ignoring their material circumstances—as, indeed, the staging does by removing furniture from the stage. Seen another way, this is a play about a woman made less defiant than her archetype by a century of social progress. Stone resurrects a female stereotype that resonates with a lot of very old attitudes—indeed, without presenting anything contrary to challenge these attitudes.

The blank staging presented nothing to challenge Her worldview—nothing to imply that there were other ways of seeing the world. The only impediments to behaving as she does are the couple's joint fertility and eventual running out of money; there is nothing to indicate that she changes her mind or learns to consider different viewpoints. Were this a play depicting characters with restricted opportunities or bleak lives, such omissions might be understandable. But there is nothing in Her life to suggest that she might not be all but tripping over opportunities to reconsider her actions. Her privilege provides her with rope to hang herself but the play does not show the costs of this to anyone else. She is offered option after option by the other characters. She settles instead on a pure egoism that finally retreats into itself.

For one scene the house appears fully furnished. For the most part, however, the play takes place on a completely bare, carpeted stage, placed within a glass box. Removing furniture so suddenly emphasises the characters over their setting. The house becomes an abstract, more universal object of desire. Without any specific detail, the "three floors" that She and John brag about to each other seem more like a trophy—something to mention offhandedly to guests—rather than something they put to any concrete use. Furniture speaks: it anchors a production in a particular time and place, hinting at a wider world beyond what is presented onstage. Here this wider world can appear and disappear as the production wishes it—a decision further emphasised by the choice to black itself out between scenes, hiding the stagehands or actors who put the furniture on and remove it. Props push back against the psychology of the characters onstage. Furniture and clothing require other people: dry cleaners, repairers, and sales assistants. Such people might come from a variety of backgrounds and classes; they might hint, however faintly, at experiences beyond those of the main characters. Any of these might be a way out of the bubble; all of them disappear. This allows the staging to focus on Piper's character. Indeed, one of the few things to mark the sides of the glass set is the vomit she spews up while drunk at a festival. The contents of her stomach receive more attention than those of her neighbourhood.

This restriction of perspective to the immediate interests of a late-1930s household involves sacrificing a lot of wider perspectives, including female bodily autonomy. Her assistant, Des, discovers that Piper's character has had an abortion in her early twenties. Abortion becomes proleptic dramatic irony: better procreate when you can, or you won't be able to later. *Yerma* does not argue against the restriction of abortion as such. However, it also shows a household torn up by a character's regret over having one. The abortion that the main character had earlier in life now comes back to haunt her. In her first scene in the play, Des tries to remember if she has had unprotected sex the night before, and if she will need a morning-after pill: "Why aren't you on the pill? / DES: . . . No it fucks with my whole aura" (31). The morning-after pill Des will eventually acquire is fraught with dramatic irony. Des is at a different stage in female sexuality as depicted within the play: the inadvertent-pregnancy years, rather than the unable-to-conceive years. John remarks to Her on how rapidly this shift has occurred: "Two years ago you'd make me wear a condom, even when you were on the pill. To make double sure" (24). This decision forms a part of the sort of choric irony around Her as a character: a warning against abortion, even one that allowed a character to have the life she wanted.

This older understanding of the procreative purposes of the household coheres with Her punishment for having sex outside of it. During "the Descent," as the simulcast's title cards referred to one scene, She seeks to have sex with two different men at the Glastonbury Festival. Strobed lighting and intensified sound design frame this as a serious, potentially extremely dangerous event. These interruptions to naturalism raised the stakes of this event past what it might reasonably be expected to bear. People—even married people—have casual sex, even chemically motivated, all the time. John has already confessed that, drunk, he had sex with a co-worker. Des has confessed to doing more or less the same thing. It is striking that in 2018 only a post-30 woman's decision to have casual sex is treated with strobe lighting and pulsing music: with the sort of interrupted motion, in other words, that suggests significant, potentially life-changing actions are occurring. This event is only as shocking as it is staged within a very lockstop understanding of lives and particularly women's lives. The consequences of her weekend at Glastonbury are approximately what they would have been in the 1890s: her husband divorces her, and she loses her house. *Yerma's* is a contemporary world in which one can still wind up at a fallen woman, on the path to suicide.

She falls in her own eyes, as well: specifically, a fall away from normalcy. It is not that she loses faith in her ideals; rather, she cannot live up to them. Her fantasy of the child is one of overwhelming normalcy—indeed, the very 2017 dramatising of a "right" to be "normal" by the classes already in power. The play's opening scene showed two middle-class white people defying political correctness, daring anyone to do anything about it. Here, she announces she wants something similar for her child:

Her: When I imagine our child I imagine it's a boy. With that cheeky look of yours like what's going on inside his mind is much much naughtier than he would ever let out. But when he gets scared he has to come here. Here against my thigh, and burrow in.

(49)

"Cheeky's" prominence in contemporary English culture requires some unpacking. Originally connoting something subversive said in a slightly "cunning way," "cheeky" first expanded into a bloated, sprawling, overused term for general laddishness: the mostly unimaginative way that entitled young men piss around in public.[15] The widespread admiration of laddishness in the UK has led to the term's general spread throughout the culture. Cheekiness often takes the form of the irritation offered up by white people doing something a bit illicit in public, knowing they're going to get away with it: young men drinking on the Underground, despite the ban, daring anyone to intervene. She announces that she wants her child to be part of the cheeky classes: those whose public self-fashioning displaces those of others. The desires of a class doing more or less as it wishes have obliterated the other stories that might have been told in this house by those groups that She and John mention: by lesbians, by minorities, or even by the average working class.

Instead, finance wins. As a repossessed property, the house will revert back to the bank. This central family's assets will disperse to the fertility and banking industries—they are still in arrears to both when the play concludes. A great deal of money has been made by these couples' travails, but it will not be realised in any tangible form, be it in their family or their neighbourhood. The bank is hedged, making money if the couple continue to make mortgage payments and making money if they default and another buyer—at a higher price—can be found. Of course, there are other ways to respond to this spiral—for example, by having contact with different ways of thinking, whether in person or in books. This can't happen here: in *Yerma*, no one talks to anyone who isn't like them.

The main character's descent into herself becomes a retreat from the wider ethical claims even of citizenship and nationhood. Piper's character's mother, for example, claims to have hated pregnancy: "HELEN: I hated the idea of getting pregnant. Being colonised by someone's sperm. Eugh. You know that film *Alien?*" (33). John's business meetings—which keep him from missing ovulation targets—are frequently in Tel Aviv. Helen is Scottish, speaking of colonialism on a London stage; of all of the countries in the world, John is doing business with Israel, site of a web of vexed colonialisms. The middle-class homeowning family's reproductive decisions become the centre of a mode of quotidian national life that is beamed around the world—to audiences that, because of simulcasting's nature, could not push back on the central performance.

This receptive class homogeneity was also visible in newspaper reviews of the play, suggesting (alongside the impossibility of getting tickets) that it struck a chord with mainstream theatregoers. I've been quoting outsider theatre critics—bloggers, mostly—throughout this piece, because it seemed like these were the primary dissenting voices around *Yerma*. Although newspapers of all political persuasions lined up to love this play, those on the right were particularly receptive to the play's story of infertility. The reliably clickbait-friendly *Mail Online*, for example, called it "a tale for all ages," comparing the performance to "Medea, Lady Macbeth, King Lear himself."[16] The free-outside-stations *Evening Standard*, although (accurately) noting the main characters' "glib remarks about the politics of gentrification" in the first scene, nevertheless also writes that "the anxieties they entertain are wholly plausible."[17] This is problem with myths: by their very definition, they contain old ideas, not all of which are worth keeping around. It's not inconceivable that a woman living in 2017 might feel about fertility in this way, with so limited a perspective on it. Nevertheless, not showing any other perspectives on that fertility, nor even giving comic relief to the sheer melodramatic weight of how the main character thinks about it, does something akin to what She and John do in their first scene together: put a progressive face on extremely regressive ideas. As Megan Vaughan writes,

> For millennia women have been degraded and belittled by men linking femininity with madness—quack doctors diagnosing "Hysteria", the trope of the "mad cat lady" (unfailingly childless), everyone who's ever asked if you're "on your period or something" after you've responded appropriately to the fact they're a fuckwit. Regardless of the individual truth of any one person's experience, theatre—or any art—which perpetuates this myth is as unforgivable as a person of colour being presented as inherently slow-witted.[18]

So near as I could tell, this particular line of critique did not make it into the major newspapers: Vaughan is a well-known blogger, but without a regular paid gig.

Yerma's newspaper reviews also praised the depth of the performance's embodiment, but do not reflect on the social world it invokes. Many reviews mention how "exhausted" Piper looked at the end of the performance.[19] Her body was praised for its commitment: for looking terrible by the end of the night, for burning itself up, and for precisely the sort of totally bodily commitment that her character sustains through her multiple rounds of IVF. The play, and the wider phenomenon of its reception, both tie women down to total commitment to the drama of childbearing.

Both Piper's character and her husband are seemingly driven out of their minds by her fertility treatments—or this, at least, is what its reviewers seemed to revere, the committed qualities of their performances. In the absence of their volition, what winds up controlling them, finally, are the extra-human actors of global finance. The play shows how unimportant any given human is to finance's colonising of a neighbourhood. They are the shock troops of gentrification: they buy their house, raising its value by improving it and by attracting others of their class to their neighbourhood. They then destroy themselves, stop making mortgage payments, and have their house revert to the bank. Annie McLanahan notes a shift in credit instruments in these last 15 years, as the central motivator of financialisation has shifted from individual banks set within countries to the "far-flung investors" of international credit markets.[20] As she suggests, "credit serves as the means through which capital extends itself in periods of growth and renews itself in moments of crisis."[21] In times of crisis, such as the housing crisis that the play reflects on, credit requires individuals to assume more of its burdens. It requires them to perform harder: precisely the sort of intensity lauded in the actors' performances. The play shows the characters losing their ability to gain any sort of critical hold on their situation. The staging's furniture—the characters' link to wider reality—disappears. They see only each other and themselves; they are locked as pure individuals within a debt-financed arena of bodily performance.

Finally, Her body is not up to the task. In this final argument, John reveals the extent of the attempts: ten rounds of IVF and massive private expenditure: "We're sixty thousand pounds in debt. Sixty. Thousand. Pounds. We're going to lose the fucking house please I'm begging please please please just stop" (74). Financialisation relies on more things becoming securities—like this couple's house, used as collateral on these debt payments. Dealing with debt leaves neither character able to say what they are thinking or what they want. This final scene hinges on an abstraction: "You didn't believe in it," she accuses him, and he agrees that he didn't (85). What "it" is—a child in the first play, a child after conception was difficult, their marriage itself—is never clarified. John was simply sceptical: aware enough of their situation to have doubts. In Her mind his biggest sin was simply being a bit hesitant about all-consuming self-destruction.

On a different sort of play, in a different sort of staging, John might have been the natural centre for our sympathies: either as comic relief or simply as a source of wise advice. She rejects John because he didn't follow him down to her ruin. He attempts to restore her decisions to her particular time and place: "[Y]ou always loved projects and you'd always been such a high achiever and God forbid you didn't achieve this." He reminds her that what feels like her own initiative has been developed in tandem with social pressures: no one becomes a "high achiever" without someone to set benchmarks. But she finally drives him from the stage: "GET OUT GET OUT GET OUT I'LL FUCKING KILL YOU GET OUT" (85). Nothing less than total commitment—of the sort that the actors were praised for—would match appropriately with this staging. John's hesitation pushes him offstage.

In the end she chooses suicide, as opposed to the husband's murder that ends Lorca's play. Indeed neither Stone's *Yerma's* nor Cusk's *Medea* allows their heroines the murders they were permitted in their original versions. She has lost her job, her house, and her husband; she finally takes her own life. The knife wound is staged graphically: she grunts and writhes, finally expiring at the back of the stage. The play's audience would have seen this from a variety of different perspectives, depending on where their seats were. In the simulcast we see only her face—deprived of the abstracting possibility of seeing her less expressive back. One of the last things She says is "No more wondering" (88). More than anything else it is stability that she has desired: to get what she wants, in other words, without complications. Stabbing herself with the knife is the final literalisation of the inward turn of her thoughts.

I thought back, finally, to those nineteenth-century domestic problem plays, dutifully staged under a proscenium arch, to which *Yerma* is a present-day heir. I have no particular nostalgia for the casually racist, restrictively sexist, unimaginably class-bound world of those plays. And yet, those nineteenth-century plays would at least have shown the members of multiple classes—maids and servants—in a tradition that went back to Shakespeare: friends and multiple generations of a family. What *Yerma* incorporates from the plays of the 1960s that decisively ended the reign of the nineteenth-century drama was its call for sexual liberation—but not these plays' accompanying call for social inclusivity. As in a tragedy, the plot's central action destroys its main character, but first, the play destroys the grounds on which other sorts of characters might take part in such an action in the first place. The anxieties of the property-owning classes had driven everyone else from the stage.

Notes

1 Simon Stone, *Yerma* (London: Oberon Books, 2017), 14. All citations are to this edition and are cited parenthetically.
2 Kim Solga and Joanne Tompkins, "The Environment of Theatre: Home in the Modern Age," in *A Cultural History of Theatre in the Modern Age*, ed. Kim Solga (London: Bloomsbury Methuen Drama, 2017), 85–88.
3 Victoria Sadler, "Review: Bodies, Royal Court," www.victoriasadler.com (blog), July 14, 2017, www.victoriasadler.com/bodies-royal-court/.
4 Alison Stone, "Not Making a Movie: The Livecasting of Shakespeare Stage Productions by The Royal National Theatre and The Royal Shakespeare Company," *Shakespeare Bulletin* 34, no. 4 (2016): 636.
5 Simon Stone, *Yerma* (London: National Theatre Live, August 30, 2017).
6 Frederico Garcia Lorca, *Yerma*, trans. Anthony Weigh (London: Faber and Faber, 2011). All citations are to this edition and are provided parenthetically.
7 Kimberly Ramírez, "*Yerma* (review)," *Theatre Journal* 60, no. 2 (2008): 298–300, 288.
8 Kathrine Ryder, "Lorca and the Gay World," *The New Yorker*, March 19, 2009, www.newyorker.com/books/page-turner/lorca-and-the-gay-world.
9 Jana Perkovic, "The Wild Duck: The Slapified Ibsen," *Guerilla Semiotics* (blog), February 25, 2012, http://guerrillasemiotics.com/2012/03/the-wild-duck-the-slapified-ibsen-reviewessay/.
10 Jane Croft, "Deliveroo Riders Not Entitled to Collective Bargaining, Court Rules," *Financial Times* (London), 2018, www.ft.com/content/51fb5da8-f879-11e8-af46-2022a0b02a6c.
11 Izabella Kaminska, "Deliveroo Announces 'Click and Collect'," *Financial Times* (London), February 27, 2019, https://ftalphaville.ft.com/2019/02/27/1551275075000/Deliveroo-announces--click-and-collect-/.
12 "IVF—a Dynamic, Innovative and Growing Market in the UK," *LaingBuisson* (press release), May 21, 2018, www.laingbuisson.com/blog/ivf-a-dynamic-innovative-and-growing-market-in-the-uk/.
13 *Avalanche* (2019, Royal Exchange/Barbican), also concerned a woman whose life unravels around attempting to have a child. *Bodies* (Royal Court, 2017) addressed international surrogacy. Both of these plays contain a moment where a character considers, and rejects, adoption.
14 Michael Billington, "Yerma Review—Billie Piper Gives a Breathtakingly Uninhibited Performance," *The Guardian* (London), August 5, 2016, www.theguardian.com/stage/2016/aug/05/yerma-review-billie-piper-young-vic-simon-stone-lorca.
15 "Cheeky," *Urbandictionary.com*, October 3, 2017, www.urbandictionary.com/define.php?term=cheeky.
16 Libby Purves, "Billie Piper's Intensity Nails the Anguish of Childlessness," *The Mail Online* (London), August 5, 2016, www.dailymail.co.uk/tvshowbiz/article-3724735/Billie-Piper-s-intensity-nails-anguish-childlessness-LIBBY-PURVES-night-review-Yerma.html.
17 Henry Hitchings, "Yerma, Theatre Review: Billie Piper Is Devastatingly Good in This Radical Reimagining of Lorca's Poetic Tragedy," *The Evening Standard* (London), 2016, www.standard.co.uk/go/london/theatre/yerma-theatre-review-billie-piper-is-devastatingly-good-in-this-radical-reimagining-of-lorcas-poetic-a3312561.html.

18   Meghan Vaughan, "On Yerma," *Synonyms for Churlish* (blog), March 10, 2016, https://synonymsforchurlish.com/on-yerma-60f0eed423e7.
19   " 'People Are Seeking out the Theatrical Experience': Brendan Cowell on Yerma's Runaway Success," *SBS News*, 2017, www.sbs.com.au/news/people-are-seeking-out-the-theatrical-experience-brendan-cowell-on-yerma-s-runaway-success.
20   Annie McClanahan, *Dead Pledges* (Palo Alto: Stanford University Press, 2016), 7.
21   Ibid., 12.

Works cited

Billington, Michael. "Yerma Review—Billie Piper Gives a Breathtakingly Uninhibited Performance." *The Guardian* (London), 2016. www.theguardian.com/stage/2016/aug/05/yerma-review-billie-piper-young-vic-simon-stone-lorca.
Brett Mason. " 'People Are Seeking out the Theatrical Experience': Brendan Cowell on Yerma's Runaway Success." *SBS News*, September 2, 2017. www.sbs.com.au/news/people-are-seeking-out-the-theatrical-experience-brendan-cowell-on-yerma-s-runaway-success.
"Cheeky." *Urbandictionary.com*. 2017. www.urbandictionary.com/define.php?term=cheeky.
Croft, Jane. "Deliveroo Riders Not Entitled to Collective Bargaining, Court Rules." *Financial Times* (London), 2018. www.ft.com/content/51fb5da8-f879-11e8-af46-2022a0b02a6c.
Garcia Lorca, Frederico. *Yerma*. Translated by Anthony Weigh. London: Faber, 2011.
Hitchings, Henry. "Yerma, Theatre Review: Billie Piper Is Devastatingly Good in This Radical Reimagining of Lorca's Poetic Tragedy." *The Evening Standard* (London), 2016. www.standard.co.uk/go/london/theatre/yerma-theatre-review-billie-piper-is-devastatingly-good-in-this-radical-reimagining-of-lorcas-poetic-a3312561.html.
"IVF—a Dynamic, Innovative and Growing Market in the UK." *LaingBuisson* (press release), May 21, 2018. www.laingbuisson.com/blog/ivf-a-dynamic-innovative-and-growing-market-in-the-uk/.
Kaminska, Izabella. "Deliveroo Announces 'Click and Collect'." *Financial Times* (London), February 27, 2019. https://ftalphaville.ft.com/2019/02/27/1551275075000/Deliveroo-announces-click-and-collect-/.
McClanahan, Annie. *Dead Pledges*. Palo Alto: Stanford University Press, 2016.
Perkovic, Jana. "The Wild Duck: The Slapified Ibsen." *guerilla semiotics* (blog), February 25, 2012. http://guerrillasemiotics.com/2012/03/the-wild-duck-the-slapified-ibsen-reviewessay/.
Purves, Libby. "Billie Piper's Intensity Nails the Anguish of Childlessness." *The Mail Online* (London), August 5, 2016. www.dailymail.co.uk/tvshowbiz/article-3724735/Billie-Piper-s-intensity-nails-anguish-childlessness-LIBBY-PURVES-night-review-Yerma.html.
Ryder, Kathrine. "Lorca and the Gay World." *The New Yorker*, March 19, 2009. www.newyorker.com/books/page-turner/lorca-and-the-gay-world.
Sadler, Victoria, "Review: Bodies, Royal Court." www.victoriasadler.com (blog), July 14, 2017. www.victoriasadler.com/bodies-royal-court/.
Solga, Kim, and Joanne Tompkins. "The Environment of Theatre: Home in the Modern Age." In *A Cultural History of Theatre in the Modern Age*, edited by Kim Solga, 75–94. London: Bloomsbury Methuen Drama, 2017.

Stone, Alison. "Not Making a Movie: The Livecasting of Shakespeare Stage Productions by the Royal National Theatre and the Royal Shakespeare Company." *Shakespeare Bulletin* 34, no. 4 (2016): 627–43.

Stone, Simon. *Yerma*. London: National Theatre Live, 30 August 2017.

———. *Yerma*. London: Oberon Books, 2017.

Vaghaun, Meghan. "On Yerma." *Synomyms for Churlish* (blog), March 10, 2016. https://synonymsforchurlish.com/on-yerma-60f0eed423e7.

Conclusion

Wanting more

Consent (2017) by Nina Raine
Harold Pinter Theatre, SW1Y 4DN
11 July 2018

Lane:	. . . I have only been married once. That was in consequence of a misunderstanding between myself and a young person.
Algernon:	[Languidly.] I don't know that I am much interested in your family life, Lane.
Lane:	No, sir; it is not a very interesting subject. I never think of it myself.

Oscar Wilde, *The Importance of Being Earnest* (1895), act one

In this exchange between the foppish Algernon and his butler Lane, Wilde grants the latter a sudden, intriguing presence within the play: one compounded, rather than foreclosed, by Algernon's languid lack of interest in the subject. Lane is given a moment to play with the sort of paradox—marriage as "a misunderstanding"—that the play's upper-class characters have enjoyed. Although in no sense is the social order overturned, Algernon and Lane seem alike aware of its surfaces. Whose performances attract attention, and what presences are suggested, on this austerity-era stage?

It's July 2018—and I'm back in the West End, at the Harold Pinter, for more of the same. We've had a year dominated by #metoo—a social movement against widespread sexual harassment and rape—in conversation with the serial outrages of the Trump administration. Nina Raine's play *Consent* started at the National Theatre last year; I'm catching it at the Harold Pinter Theatre, formerly the Comedy, about a block off Haymarket Street. And *Consent* is this book's argument in miniature. A middle-class love quadrilateral takes place, awkwardly, against the barely there backdrop of a rape trial. Kitty and Edward are lawyers, married to one another; Tim is Edward's friend, a single lawyer who has just (it's London in 2017) bought a house with high ceilings; Zara is an actress who wants a baby. Over the course of the play Kitty and Edward will have an argument; Tim and Zara, a relationship; and Kitty and Tim, an affair.

The play's main characters are all hard-charging legal types: the London elite. Or, we might say, *a* London elite: when I saw the production, all of the characters were white, and all had variegated middle-class accents. (Priyanga Burford, a lone South Asian actress who played Rachel in the initial cast, had been replaced by Sian Clifford, who is white, in the West End transfer.) We are I believe meant to see their casual cruelty as bracing: part of the cost of toiling in the wheels of the just society, and even a sign of their ethical decay as a result. The play leaves open to the audience the opportunity to read these characters as crass and unpleasant, detached from those they are supposed to serve. And yet the play itself is analogously indifferent to any characters who do not come from this tight ring of privileged London backgrounds. So Edward will note a divorce case involving "a Tamil stabbing his wife . . . He ran off to the Bahamas and came back with a tattoo on his arm that said 'Forgive and forget'" (62). The characters onstage find this funny. Yet *Consent* gives that unnamed "Tamil" no opportunity to show that he is anything other than a violent throwaway joke.

It is a matter of attention and interest. *Consent*, like many plays, flatters its audience's savoir-faire about London. We don't need to have explained to us the significance of Rachel's clue that her husband is cheating on her, a receipt for " 'One Prawn Sandwich, Paddington M&S.' But he hates prawn sandwiches" (41). The play substantiates this sort of small detail, showing it extending into the web of its plot; the Tamil and his tattoo are a punchline.

These characters engage in the same sort of bodily competition that defined the main character in *Yerma*. They talk openly and explicitly about their sex lives and matters of reproductive health with hedonistic zest, in a way that shows them as strong individuals rather than as part of a health care system, as when Kitty discusses giving birth:

Kitty: Yes. When the GP saw him, he said—(*Tones of awe.*) 'Was he *vaginal?*'
Jake: God.—And was he?
Kitty: *Yes!*
Jake: Respect.

(8)[1]

Here again we note a broader tendency against collective forms of identification. Kitty addresses her childbirth as a feat of athleticism, which she undertook alone, receiving praise but not particularly assistance from doctors. Like the female character in *Yerma* describing her pelvic floor, Kitty describes her health in terms of private achievement rather than public service.

As in *Yerma*, these descriptions edge into descriptions of sexual violence. The conceit of the opening scene is that we slowly learn that Edward and Jake are lawyers, respectively defending and prosecuting rapists. Rape, and the justice system more generally, provides an opportunity for several sorts of social performance. It affords these characters rooms with high windows, clever things to say at parties, and even (in Ed's case) the chance to indulge a hobby for accents:

Kitty: Ed's so heartless. He just thinks there's another good accent for me to do. Like the Geordie paedophile.

Edward: Oh, he was brilliant value. *(Puts on a Geordie accent in a very high-pitched voice.)* 'I'm telling you, I didn't do it, this will ruin my life, please, you've got to believe me!' *(Reverting to own voice.)* Anyway what's interesting in *this* case is that I'm incredibly promiscuous as well as being a rapist. All these Sharons and Traceys keep coming out of the woodwork. You know, one of the coppers in the case was actually shagging me?

(14)

We have at the bottom of this hierarchy the "Sharons and Traceys": interchangeable women, who come "out of the woodwork"—like insects—when a rape case appears in court. Next we have the rapist himself, a figure of "interest": he has a regional accent, and an "incredibly promiscuous love life," something extraordinary. And finally we have the middle-class solicitor, capable of emulating all of these figures: of ventriloquizing how they speak outside of court, suggesting the control over their discourse he holds within it.

Consent shows the very architecture of the city, its walls, and buildings, via *class capture*. The sole court case is presented entirely in terms of Edward and Jake's exchanges with one another. This is class capture as a staging decision: we see two middle-class characters along with a character of an unspecified other, lower class—with regional accent to boot—interacting with them. We do not see the other people who would be involved in the courtroom: the judge, the members of the jury, courtroom clerks, and so on forward. The presence onstage of these characters might ground the courtroom scene in some sort of wider social reality—and, in doing so, might diminish somewhat Edward and Jake's impact on the scene.

Consent presents even the most basic elements of human experience and mutual empathy as up for argument. However, the architectonics of this argument—the way it is present onstage—coheres with characters of a particular class. Within this framework, mostly unmoored (with the sole exception of Gayle's presence) from the presence of others, arguments attain a plausibility that they might not otherwise. Edward has built up his moral *bona fides*, the play claims, by work as a human rights lawyer and now representing poorer victims. Yet he does not express much empathy with them. Indeed, he will claim at another of the play's party scenes, "in my experience, the *victims* were never completely innocent either. I'm fed up with them. They're all mad. No smoke without fire. They're like the weird bullied people at school" (61). "School" is of course where you pick up an accent like Edward's. Edward excludes himself from the bullied; indeed, from his short haircut, we can surmise he was one of the sporty types (or at least is attempting to remain so now.) His mindset is one whose cockpit remains those school years.

Poor Gayle is not a competitor. She really doesn't stand much of a chance as an onstage presence. The middle-class characters are dismissive even of the veracity of her claim. Their discussion leaves open the possibility that Gayle was not actually raped—that she was, as Edward describes her, "a complete pisshead who kept changing her story" (43). Against this account we have Gayle's own sympathetic presence. Yet characters will present arguments that foreclose this small space of compelling empathy further.

Edward: Not empathy, not that old fucking chestnut, please—
Kitty: Ed—
Edward: —I'm so sick of hearing that word invoked! . . . It's completely *innu-merate*, for a start. . . . A genocide doesn't get as much attention as one little boy killed and hidden in someone's attic.

(56)

Again, within the argumentative toolkit the play offers to its audience, it would be possible to discard Gayle entirely: as either an outright liar; a victim who (like those bullied in school, in Edward's account) brought her attack on herself; or simply as a disproportionate recipient, her status a rape victim in England giving her a status over the victims of a genocide. The play's staging seems to reflect this logic. Numerically Gayle is outnumbered by her social superiors. She has no onstage peer, at least in class terms. And her presence is rationed out by the playwright: she appears in three scenes, in all of which she is (not unreasonably) distraught. We know nothing about her life other than her accent and her status as a victim: not her job, not her place of origin other than what we associate with her accent. This seems like a textbook case of the "psychosocial dynamics" that would exclude working-class people from the theatre.[2]

To combat this, *Consent* might have made a disproportionate case for Gayle— indeed, 60 years ago, a play like *Roots* might have. The technical dynamics of the stage, lighting and sound, might have been aligned with her sensory experience as a rape victim. Here, however, as the *New York Times* critic Matt Wolf writes, "Ms. Raine sells short . . . the working-class Gayle (Heather Craney), whose rape exists to illustrate the intractability of the very institutions that Tim, Edward and their like navigate with ease."[3] Gayle is reduced to her barest elements, an impossible-to-verify story and a regional accent, as she is demolished in court: EDWARD. . . . Did you take a drink to bed with you? / GAYLE. . . . I dinnae remember (33). She subsequently crashes the main characters' party, revealing that her sister had killed herself because of an earlier rape that the two shared. She explains that she had been in therapy at the time of her alleged rape:

'Cause I was *raped*, that's why. Years before. Before Patrick Taylor. Me and my sister hitchiking, two blokes, picked us up and took us to the wood. They did us side by side. / That's why I was *having* therapy. Ten years later. *Because* I was raped . . . I held her hand while it was going on.

(71)

Paul Taylor, reviewing the play in the *Independent*, demotes this second rape to a "violent assault."[4] And indeed the particularities of Gayle's case do not truly seem to matter. Throughout the scene, various characters have played with a knife used to peel an apple; by Chekovian expectations, our attentions drift towards its potential for violence. Yet nothing happens. Gayle leaves the party without doing anything. Her only violence is self-directed: a scene later, we find out in dialogue that she has hanged herself.

Cruelly, it is also hanging objects that establish where the play's scenes are taking place. To reflect the various London locales in which the play takes place, the set design raises and lowers a set of lightshades. In this way, the play implies, the various interiors coexist. Yet Gayle is accorded no lampshade—and so no room—of her own. Where she lives does not matter for the action of the play. The setting gives a version of London that spotlights the affluent private homes of a few, rather than anything like a plurality of the experiences that the city contains.

Instead, Gayle haunts those who live in nicer interiors. This seems the central moral: that the abuse of characters like Gayle supports these middle-class edifices. Following Gayle's suicide, Tim's new town house begins to show the signs of a ghost:

Tim: The upstairs landing, I was looking around it, and I found these . . . marks low down on the wall.
Kitty: What kind of marks?
Tim: Little . . . it looked like little finger marks. . . . I'd just had it painted.

(50)

The tactility of these markings suggests the hand-holding of Gayle's rape. Yet even in giving this account of his house's haunting by the circumstances of his job, Tim cannot help but describe himself as the sort of person who would not do that painting himself. Further, this scene leads to the beginning of his affair with Kitty. This leads to some difficulties in Kitty's relationship with Edward, but at the close of the play, things seem possibly ironed out between them. Things have a funny way of working out for the middle-class characters, and the play presents little to suggest there is not a sort of rightness to this.

Even Gayle's ghost accedes to this point of view. When she reappears, she is entirely "dispassionate," as the stage directions inform us. This is also the word used by Edwards as he describes why "victims shouldn't have a role in punishment" (25). Following her death, Gayle seems to have acceded to this position: she can view the character economy that her interlocking story of rape and eventual suicide has with "dispassion," removed from her stake in the matter. The stage leaves it open to the audience how she is to be interpreted, but the script seems to indicate that she has moved on from the troubling matters of her rape and suicide. As an audience surrogate, Gayle's ghost shows that what has happened to her, her own humiliation after serial rape, is somehow manageable—or, worse, that it is a little bit troubling, a fingerprint on the wall. The rape is not staged; neither is Gayle's death; neither, indeed, is any moment of her life away from the middle-class characters. She is described as a spectral presence haunting the play's central cast of middle-class lawyers, described entirely in terms of her impact on their lives. And what this impact is is never stated. The characters never look at her ghost; they never mention her past a certain point in the play.

It is the work of theatre and of other artistic forms to potentially jar us out of this quiescence. Yet *Consent* shows this worldview even colonising the theatre, adjusting the jarring universals of Greek theatre in order to reinforce the stabilising machine of the London middle-class stage. Zara is an actress who has been in a play that resembles the Rachel Cusk *Medea* that I describe in my introduction. This flirts with metatheatricality: with a winking awareness, shared with the audience, of the inherent staginess of its setting. Zara assumes her hosts have a shaggy awareness of Greek drama, at least for cocktail party purposes: "KITTY. What's the play like? / ZARA. Well, you know. It's Greek." (21) The characters go on to address Greek plays in familiarising terms:

Edward:　They're just fundamentally unpleasant people, aren't they?
Tim:　The men are shits and the women are insufferable because they're so holier-than-thou. Right?

(21)

As in the *Cusk* Medea, the emotional intensity of these Greek characters, and the potentially larger-than-normal ideals with which they contend, are localised: in Tim's speech to annoying personality traits. The key to these dramas, Tim believes, is that "Two opposing characters holding two relative but mutually destructive truths. (*The wine.*) Can I have a bit more of that?" (22). This is Georg Wilhem Friedrich Hegel's conception of tragedy: that such a clash leads to the eventual progress of society as a whole, a "spirit" that extends across the whole of a nation.[5] For Tim, however, there is no general progress: the significant thing is the clash that pays his bills, and the wine he gets as a reward—a product that, not insignificantly, is sold in the lobby. And the only spirit here is that of an outsider faintly intruding on a set of middle-class interiors.

It may be that all of the play's characters hold "relative" truths that cause destruction to one another—even if, as I have noted, the "destruction" caused to the middle-class characters is a temporarily relationship wobble. But no Greek tragedy would ignore that characters also experience non-equivalent burdens—any more so than Hegel misses the suffering created by the clash of competing tragic worldviews. Instead *Consent* shows these characters asserting ownership—as the Arts Council suggests they should—over these Greek narratives and the universality of experience towards which they gesture.

Their invocation of Greek tragedy seems to invite the destructive force of Nemesis, yet in the end the central relationship seems on its way to being saved. At the very least, the middle-class characters have learned to feel empathy—but only for each other. In the production that I saw, at the final moment the actors fell into the clash the stage directions called for. Kitty tells Edward "you're making me feel sorry for you," and the following occurs:

Kitty: *tries to pull him up. It doesn't work. Slowly she gets down and kneels in front of him. Their hands are on each other's shoulders—half-grapple, half-embrace. Silently, GAYLE's ghost appears at the back of the room, where she stood at the start of the play. She watches them. Fade to black.*

(102)

When I saw the production, a slow last tableau had these characters circling their heads around each other, moving towards this final potential embrace, which—whatever its outcome—portends nothing as damaging as a hanging. The slow kindling of empathy that results from the close observation of two silent bodies does not happen for Gayle, whose offstage hanging becomes simply "watching" the main characters as a ghost—an audience surrogate. Her life is like our lives, in thrall to these clever lawyers.

Indeed, Gayle is not even granted the exclusive right to a body for the duration of the performance. The script is insistent that "Gayle and Laura," the divorce attorney that Kitty and Edward consult, "should be doubled" (7). This transformation occurs in the second half of the play, which instructs us "The same actress who played GAYLE, who now speaks in RP, as LAURA, a solicitor, sits with KITTY" (85). The play is canny about the ways that accent gives one control over a situation: the difference between Gayle's "strong Scottish accent" and Laura's RP is the difference between being a rape victim and a successful attorney (17). Yet even for England this casual whizzing about of class positions and accents feels Manichean: to state the obvious, one can be both Scottish (or simply have a regional accent) and be a lawyer, or speak in RP and be a rape victim. Moreover, this is a failure of the play's attention. This doubling implies that Gayle's character matters less than her function within the play—she serves, in the words of Natasha Tripney's again mostly positive review, "as little more than a dramatic catalyst—a source of disruption" to the "relationships" the lawyer characters have with one another.[6]

To consider why these critics kept overlooking this class component, consider the arts ecosystem in which the play appears: specifically, the way newspaper reviewers framed the play. Writing in 2007 about the theatre of the previous decade, Andrew Haydon notes that "The first-string critics for all the major broadsheets, were white, middle-class, mostly Oxbridge-educated men with conservative tastes in theatre".[7] He does note the promising possibilities of Lyn Gardner's blog pieces, which, as he notes, often serve as a "re-review" of Michael Billington, their primary critic. A decade later, the situation was unchanged—only the *Guardian* has fired Lyn Gardner.[8] Following Billington's retirement in 2019, he was replaced by Arifa Akbar—there is indeed now a female first-string critic writing for a major English broadsheet. Yet for the period this book reviews, this was not the case—and this coverage of *Consent* reveals the limitations of having a frankly patriarchal coterie of reviewers attending to productions about subjects like rape. Gendered praise for the play came thick and fast: Dominic Cavendish, writing for the *Daily Telegraph,* writes that Raine has "given birth to a new genre"; Matt Wolf, writing for the *New York Times*, praises her "distaff" version of Patrick Marber, using a strongly gendered word for "household" I associate with the nineteenth century.[9] The reviews reveal a closed, clannish theatrical world: an offstage equivalent of the homogeneity *Consent* places onstage. Cavendish identifies the playwright as "Raine (daughter of poet Craig)," alluding to the well-known English poet who is Nina's father; he adds, "Raine's own baby Misha was good as gold at the final preview."[10]

From genesis to staging to the person who played its baby, *Consent* made the outright majority of the population who do not possess middle-class habitus seem like outliers. In the wider life that this theatre purports to address, of course, these other presences don't haunt the middle classes—they outnumber them. #metoo is not about the ghostly, flickering, occasional presence of sexual assault: it is about its prominence, its frequency, and the ways that gender abuse has been *made* to seem ghostly. *Consent* presents nothing less than an act of class and gender erasure, from the lampshades on down.

"It's good, isn't it?" the person sitting to my right said to his partner, about five minutes into the production. The audience I sat among laughed at its jokes about rape and at characters' invocation of "prep school" and expensive wines. They got the jokes about "Putney" being a déclassé suburb, and laughed on cue. The classical lite music that played between scenes gave the proceedings the air of quality. Yet, a year on from *Ink, Consent* seemed simply more of the same: mimetic humour and even empathy, making and remaking an unfair world exactly as it was in the name of quality drama. Theatre had become a luxury good—only, unlike the Veuve Cliquot in the *Ink* lobby, one that still brought with it the whiff of a social critique now so thoroughly defanged that it could be brought back as humour. This is what happens when you stress "ownership" of the theatre, as the Arts Council suggests: you invoke the extremes of human experience and turn them into a well-wrought consumer good, overseen by an enviable middle-class elite. The audience seemed to want what these characters had; the play could show what had been sacrificed to give it to them only as ghostly fingerprints on a privately owned wall.

We want more: an audience checklist

I think it's time for audiences to start demanding more. Theatre can be a truly shocking art form, nowhere more so than when it—to indulge in a vital cliché—challenges our preconceptions. There is a coziness to being told that the world was always going to be the way it turned out to be; something reassuring in having our prejudices and preconceptions about how the world works reconfirmed. But we can genuinely see the world in a new way through art, rather than just leave with a sense that things are always going to be like the way things are now.

Rather than some sort of ringing conclusion—you know what I think, by now—I'd like to suggest some hard questions that you, the global theatregoer, might productively begin to ask of theatre companies and arts venues in general. If theatre isn't doing any or all of these things, you may want to consider taking your patronage elsewhere—or, perhaps more critically, leaving the sort of informed audience feedback that might lead to real and lasting change in what gets performed on our stages.

1 Did it take me out of my comfort zone? Did I make some sort of connection with people who are different than me?

A connection does not necessarily mean that you find all of the characters totally relatable, as we say—or in particular that you approved of their actions. But were their motivations clear or interesting or in some way compelling? Did they make the difficult-to-relate-to in some way plausible? It helps to be ruthless in asking this question of yourself, and of theatres: to know who you are, what categories of people you are closest to, and which you might be furthest away from. Think in terms of double and even triple jumps: differences of race *and* class, or sexuality *and* taste. Or, even, all four together. Equally, ask if a distant setting—the past, the future—wound up seeming a lot like our present-day lives: if a Hungarian royal palace of the seventeenth century, or a mining colony on Jupiter wound up seeming like a television commercial for a big family Christmas. If the play was set in a familiar place and said familiar things about people who seemed basically familiar, you can—and should—ask more from it.

2 Was I invited to consider how society might be made different from how it is now?

Did the play invite us to consider how things might change? This does not have to mean that the play ends with a twenty-ninth-century Portuguese-speaking feminist eco-utopia (although, respect, if it managed to). Nor does it mean that a play about slavery needs to end with a rousing call to be nicer to one another. But all theatre can at least be illuminating of lingering problems: does it show us something that we keep doing that we need to stop, even in an abstract way? Does it make us aware of our blind spots? To put it even more simply, did it make you notice things in wider life you had not noticed before? If a play left you feeling helpless, or even amused, at the notion that nothing in society will ever really change, you can ask more from it.

3 Was there anything I continued to think about, months (or even years) after the performance?

Have a look at your calendar—from a year ago, or perhaps even further back. Can you remember scenes, imagines, lines of dialogue, costumes, actors, or sets from things that you saw a while ago? Do you find yourself repeating lines of dialogue with yourself? Or, even more intensely, do you find yourself wanting to talk to people about the play, even a year or so onwards—do you find it as an example you use when talking to friends? Good theatre can and should haunt you, and should particularly do so in terms of its details. One of the problems with summarising something as "a good night out" is the genericness of its description: we might have a night out at the movies, or a concert, or a bowling alley, or the mall. All of these are valid and fascinating in their own ways—but they are also very different. It's more than a bit numbing to apply something as vague as "goodness" to all of these very different experiences. If you remember a particularly well-fitting pair of jeans that you found on sale at a particular mall on an evening when you recall the unusual rain patterns outside, you've made a granular connection with an event in your life. If you go back to your calendar and remember absolutely nothing from a play that you saw—or worse, if you remember the food in the restaurant or something that happened on the bus—you can ask more from that theatre.

4 Did the creative team come from a wide range of backgrounds?

Most theatre companies give out programs listing in detail the experience of the creative team of their plays. At the very least, they'll have a cast sheet available at the theatre, or information up on their website. Have a look at the backgrounds of the actors, directors, lighting designers, and so on forward: do they all seem to come from the same handful of places, and to have trained in the same sort of schools? Are they instead from all over the country, or all over the world? A range of experiences among makers leads to theatre that is less boring. In contrast, a creative industry that comes from a homogenous range of experiences will only know to look for a homogenous range of details. There are some well-hewn clichés that can be said against this: that the truly qualified people find their way to the good programs. This is about 10% truth and 90% conformist nonsense. A lot of qualified people are kept out of the creative industries because audiences have not had a chance to resonate with the perspectives they might offer. Theatre will get better—more interesting, more idea-rich—if people from a variety of places make it. If everyone who created the play seems to be more-or-less from the same place, you can probably ask more from it. Frankly, this point is particularly critical, in our survey-driven age: if audiences don't keep pushing for more diverse companies, or imply that they prefer a lack of diversity, theatres will continue to hire the same sorts of people to make samey-seeming plays about similar situations.

5 Was there anything left unfinished, raw, rough, or uneven—and did I speculate about it?

This is the tricky one, because it might seem to be excusing a lot of bad theatre. But not all artworks need to be fully smoothed out and perfect, particularly if they're dealing with issues the wider society has not figured out either. It's a lot to ask a 90-minute play to solve, say, hepatitis, or the decline of the mining industry. But smart theatre knows this, and uses rawness to direct its audience's speculative attention. Did the gaps in the performance, did what was left unsaid or unfinished, make you think more about what was going on? In contrast, did everything seem too polished, too set, too over-rehearsed? If a performance was so self-possessed and slick that it left you with nothing to think about, you can ask hard questions about what use it was as an evening out. This doesn't mean you had to have a bad time—far from it, particularly given the way that the shock of misery has so often led to conformist pessimism in recent productions. But were you left intrigued, or numbed?

6 Did it punch up or kick down?

As humans we have an innate tendency to identify with other humans; this effect is only intensified by live performance. Theatre if it is working makes us feel deeply and intensely—and there is no particular guarantee that the power it has over us will lead to good or beneficial things. In particular, theatre can make us identify very intensely with a tiny, limited world, to the exclusion of everything outside. It can confirm our own echo chambers, hiding other sorts of perspectives and experiences. Theatre can wind up aligning with the values of the established classes—indeed this book has been a sustained argument that much theatre in London around the Brexit decision was dominated with precisely this sort of thing. Past a certain point, this ceases to be interesting: showing the winning classes winning again lacks tension or dramatic interest. This is another opportunity for audiences to be ruthless: to think about how society is, and to imagine where the characters depicted in the play sit within it. If a play shows the comfortable staying comfortable, we can ask more of it.

7 Did its set do anything, or was it just there to look pretty? Was its realism, or were its interruptions to realism, productive?

London's West End in particular is celebrated and condemned for the elaborateness of its sets, which come with a related tendency to exist for their own sake. Looking expensive becomes a way of justifying high ticket prices. But sets are at their best dynamic: they're part of the argument a play is making, resonating with the sorts of awareness the play seeks to raise or create. If the set just kind of sat there looking as though no expense had been spared in making it, you're allowed to ask for more.

8 Did it shock for a reason?

Look: we're 70 years on from when nudity or sexual violence on stage was in any sense new. This is not to say that extreme things placed on stage cannot still be shocking; just that they are no longer innately so. Certain sorts of theatre courts audience shock—walkouts, even—as a way of consolidating the viewpoint of a profitable majority of those in the audience who can feel as though they have attended something progressive, innovative, or "artistic." But ethically questionable things do still bring with them ethically questionable values when placed on a stage. If you go to the theatre frequently, extreme stuff gets pretty dull pretty quickly unless it is linked to some sort of contrast: some steady state, some consensus, for the nudity and violence to interrupt. Otherwise shock can simply present a yet-more-extreme form of the numbing sameness that theatre can promote. Audiences can and should ask more of theatres that present extremity without purpose.

9 Did it seem to favour only one kind of audience, or could you imagine it appealing to a wide range of people?

This isn't to call for theatre not to be difficult. An extremely abstract or difficult play could be equivalently baffling to all audiences—as long as it clearly isn't withholding meaning from some groups while offering it to others. Something that speaks only in the language, interests, affect, and style of one limited social group, without acknowledging the possibility of interpretation by others, is however bad theatre. Did the play make an effort to bring you into its world: to unpack things for you, or failing that to give you a way into figuring out what was happening? If not, ask for more.

10 Did the performance interact in any way with the place—the geography, the community, the country—where the theatre was?

One of the issues with the ponderous megamusicals is that, transferred once or twice away from their theatres of origin, they start to lose all connection with the actual world. There's no particular reason to see them in London, where (to be honest) your ticket is probably going to be more expensive and your seat more uncomfortable. Theatre can, alternately, interact meaningfully with the place where it is set: can adapt itself to the particular form of the theatre it's in, the particular place in the city where that theatre sits. This is perhaps the most optional of these requirements: realist theatre, for example, is premised on the idea that across the fourth wall we are being taken to a definite other time and place. But if the play evoked no particular place whatsoever, you can ask for more.

11 Did this have a reason to exist as a play? Did it take advantage of anything theatres in particular can do?

The way of all flesh for nationally prominent playwrights seems to be to head for television and the movies—and fair enough, given the precarity of arts careers and the excellence of writing for both media at the moment. Nevertheless, plays are not television or movies in embryo; theatre has its own rules, dynamics, and possibilities. If the play seemed to be playing to its live simulcast—to a global audience watching on a flat screen—more than to those of you actually in the theatre, you have every reason to demand more.

This checklist is designed to make you, the prospective London audience member, feel entitled and powerful—as indeed you are. Say what you will for Arts Council recommendations: right now, it's a buyer's market for audience feedback. This truly is, for better and for worse, a moment when your feedback can make a difference to what gets put on in the theatre. If you tell a theatre "good job" in your feedback, they're going to carry on doing precisely what it is they've always done. Focused feedback on definite aspects of the production is rare; it will be carried quickly to the highest levels of an organisation, and will produce real change. I would like to imagine a possible arts regime that does not make arts organisations dance so comprehensively to audience feedback; in the regime that we have, however, go to town. Smart audiences are always required for good theatre to happen; at the moment, we also need to be demanding.

Notes

1 Nina Raine, *Consent* (London: Nick Hern Books, 2017). All citations are by ebook page number and are given in the text.
2 BOP Consulting and Graham Devlin Associates, *Analysis of Theatre in England* (London: BOP Consulting and Graham Devlin Associates, 2016), 3.
3 Matt Wolf, "Adultery with a Difference on the London Stage," *The New York Times* (New York), April 24, 2017, www.nytimes.com/2017/04/24/theater/london-theater-consent-goat.html.
4 www.independent.co.uk/arts-entertainment/theatre-dance/consent-review-dorfman-national-theatre-london-nina-raine-a7668386.html.
5 Georg Wilhelm Friedrich Hegel, *Aesthetics: Lectures on Fine Art*, trans. T. M. Knox, 2 vols (Oxford: Clarendon, 1998), Vol. 2, 1159.
6 Paul Taylor, "*Consent*, Dorfman, National Theatre, London, Review: One of Nina Raine's Most Enjoyable and Intelligent Plays Yet," *The Independent* (London), April 5, 2017, www.thestage.co.uk/reviews/2017/consent-review-at-the-dorfman-national-theatre-london/.
7 Haydon, Andrew. "Theatre in the 2000s." In *Modern British Playwriting 2000–2009*, edited by Dan Rebellato, 40–99. London: Bloomsbury, 2013, 93.
8 Giverny Masso, "Guardian Ends Contract with Critic Lyn Gardner After 23 Years," *The Stage* (London), 2018, www.thestage.co.uk/news/2018/guardian-ends-contract-critic-lyn-gardner/.
9 Wolf, "Adultery."
10 Dominic Cavendish, "A Tense, Entertaining Modern-Day Tragi-Comedy—Consent, National's Dorfman Theatre, Review," *The Daily Telegraph* (London), April 4, 2017, www.telegraph.co.uk/theatre/what-to-see/tense-entertaining-modern-day-tragi-comedy-consent-nationals/.

Works cited

BOP Consulting and Graham Devlin Associates. *Analysis of Theatre in England*. London: BOP Consulting and Graham Devlin Associates, 2016.
Cavendish, Dominic. "A Tense, Entertaining Modern-Day Tragi-Comedy—Consent, National's Dorfman Theatre, Review." *The Daily Telegraph* (London), April 4, 2017.

www.telegraph.co.uk/theatre/what-to-see/tense-entertaining-modern-day-tragi-comedy-consent-nationals/.

Hegel, Georg Wilhelm Friedrich. *Aesthetics: Lectures on Fine Art*. Translated by T.M. Knox. 2 vols. Oxford: Clarendon, 1998, Vol. 2.

Masso, Giverny. "Guardian Ends Contract with Critic Lyn Gardner after 23 Years." *The Stage* (London), 2018. www.thestage.co.uk/news/2018/guardian-ends-contract-critic-lyn-gardner/.

Raine, Nina. *Consent*. London: Nick Hern Books, 2017.

Taylor, Paul. "*Consent*, Dorfman, National Theatre, London, Review: One of Nina Raine's Most Enjoyable and Intelligent Plays Yet." *The Independent* (London), April 5, 2017. www.thestage.co.uk/reviews/2017/consent-review-at-the-dorfman-national-theatre-london/.

Wolf, Matt. "Adultery with a Difference on the London Stage." *The New York Times*, April 24, 2017. www.nytimes.com/2017/04/24/theater/london-theater-consent-goat.html.

Afterword

Estate of the nation, *Jerusalem* to *Albion*

We've taken six relatively deep dives (as we say in 2020) into the performance cultures linked to particular London neighbourhoods. In all of them, a fixation on private property ownership triggered a withdrawal from wide public sympathy. How might we account for this within a larger history of the English stage? I've suggested how plays like Wesker's *Roots* (1958) spoke to a wider range of outcomes for people from a range of classes—a possibility that plays of this post-Brexit era showed property ownership foreclosing. Significant plays from 2009 to 2017 moved from an inclusive inventory of the country's historic multiculturalism, and towards a more exclusive accounting of what defines England against other countries. When theatre-makers of the 2010s address English nationalism, they repetitively engage with a paradigm of property ownership: one that framed English history and the English present alike as a contest between native white property-owning and property-renting classes.

Beatie Bryant came from a moment in when narratives of non-traditional classes and individuals were being considered. A signal play of the immediately post-financial-crash era was probably Jez Butterworth's *Jerusalem*, which appeared at the Royal Court in 2009.[1] It makes no secret of its state-of-the-nation play intentions, with a curtain displaying the words "the English Stage Company"—the original Royal Court company—on an on-stage amateur stage. In what follows, agents of a town council attempt to evict John "Rooster" Byron from "an old forty-foot mobile home" parked illegally in a long-term squat.[2] *Jerusalem* has been much commented on, with most reviewers mentioning Mark Rylance's performance in the central role. I didn't see it, relying instead on the script. Critics have noticed its issues, most prominently its unreflective embrace of "white straight male experience and desire" in a way that "barely nod[s] to women's existence."[3] The dominance of Rylance's stage presence appears to have exacerbated this effect.

Yet, even as it is a strongly male-centric play, *Jerusalem* as a script kicks hard against certain traditions—particularly, against an English nostalgia that might have seemed more attractive in forceful performance. Characters evoke the Blakean nostalgia of the hymn for which the play is named, and with which it opens, but the run of the plot reveals that its village's community is built on generational child neglect and sexual abuse, whose victims include the teenager who sings this hymn. Rooster is livid at "all those sorry cunts on the New Estate," a new housing development built nearby. Yet these sexual transgressions suggest that Rooster's carnivalesque resistance of the law—the "Public Health Act of 1878, and the Pollution Control and Local Government Order 1974" intoned by a council employee before he appears onstage—is something long overdue to come to an end. In performance, Rooster's conclusory listing of his ancestors may have accorded power to this possibly "feudal" understanding of the English past, in which, as April De Angelis notes, a young woman is exchanged between two violent father figures.[4] In reading, it's also possible to find this cumbersome reciting of ancient patriarchs a tearing out, root and branch, of the patterns of abuse and neglect from which they may have benefited: a listing of the deservedly dead, to which Rooster himself will soon be added.

No history can be taken à la carte—Rooster's misogyny (and, if more ambiguously, the play's) anchors them both to what was already retrograde in 2009. But at least what *Jerusalem* possibly, queasily glorified, or at least acknowledged, was also hybrid and inclusive. Its characters are proudly regional but consume global culture. They casually "bring the ruckus," not just citing American rap supremos the Wu-Tang Clan but also suggesting that rap's "global picture" of "marginality" has become part of their self-construction as contemporary Britons.[5] The unpropertied, the Wu, racism, and alcoholic rebellion are all present in this stock-taking of the English present.

Jerusalem presents a wider and more resilient account of this cultural hybridity than many plays that came after it. The antagonist to Rooster's ambitions of mythic self-sufficiency, at least as he frames them, is the "Kennet and Avon Council," who have sponsored "the New Estate": a housing development. The play leaves ambiguous whether these houses are publicly or privately owned—the history of the late 2000s suggests probably some mixture, with "Partnership between [the] public, private and voluntary sectors" typifying planning in the era.[6] Nevertheless, the presence of a town council intervening in local housing matters—not only weeding out the faeries, but also culling the drug dealers and sex pests—falls out of favour with the subsequent stage paradigm. The Rooster-Council contest holds open, for the length of the play, the possibility of alternative understandings of property ownership and of state intervention: not as compatible, but at least as co-present. Theatre following *Jerusalem* would reflect contemporary government's post-financial crash embrace of wide-spectrum practices of privatisation. As De Angelis suggests, there is no utopic past to return to—or if there is, it certainly isn't *Jerusalem's* gender politics. And yet, around property ownership and what it portends for full participation in national life, *Jerusalem* seems something of a last gasp. Subsequently a place within private property relations becomes the classifier separating the viable from the abject, the struggling from the failed. This is a recapitulation rather than a challenging of the current governmental paradigm that Imogen Tyler describes, its division of people into successes and failures.[7]

Richard Bean's *England People Very Nice* (NT, 2009) stages waves of immigration to Bethnal Green, a neighbourhood in East London, as a narrative of English self-understanding—in which every generation of immigrants buys property and then beggars the next. Like *Jerusalem, England People* is another play-within-a-play: here, a historical pageant performed by claimants waiting in a refugee processing centre. In it, the same story happens to first French, then Jewish, and then Bangladeshi immigrants. Each faces pushback against their religious and cultural observance, next experiences sexual integration, and finally garners enough local traction to begin to push back against the next wave of immigrants. Addressing the play's humour would require more space than my present project has to attempt sensitively. In a play in which every national type is wildly stereotyped, I remain cool to the play's stereotyping of its most recent migrants, those greatest at risk of being punched down to by the play's "let's frame everyone in offensive terms" satire. And yet, the play also frames the history of England as inevitably, massively hybrid—the accretion of waves after waves of immigration, each one of whom determines the spaces in which the next generation of migrants will live. And it offers a warning: at its conclusion, the framed pageant ends, and one of its performers, Iqbal, is turned down for asylum. He will be denied the chance to remain, procreate, and exploit a subsequent generation of newcomers. Property relations remain intact, but England's hybrid past is ending.

It's always tempting—and usually distortive—to make the case for snap developments in literary history: in this year, this event happened, and this play framed/refracted/reacted to it, in these ways. Plays and productions take a while to develop. But of course political ideas too are also slowly cultivated. Long-gestating concepts, theatrical and political, may find themselves stumbling together into a shared spotlight. The 2010 General Election, resulting in the Conservative-Liberal Democrat coalition government, is as good a point as any to note theatrical discourses following apparent shifts in the national mood. Ownership within a less hybrid understanding of the national past becomes normalised in many plays of the following decade, as it would be within its political discourse. Laura Wade's *Posh* (Royal Court/2010) is a fictionalisation of the Oxford eating club of which two of this decade's prime ministers were members. It opens with its characters describing the wallpaper in a private member's club in London, and will proceed as they damage a country pub, its owner, and his daughter. Its production during a general election and obviously elites-vs.-working-people politics coincided with an emerging pattern: the country figured as privately owned spaces, within which class positions remain exaggeratedly stagnant. *Posh* gives the best lines to its aristocrats. Its working characters are there to be abused, insulted, and bought off. And there are no alternatives: all characters are locked into these spaces, and into their social roles, with equivalent inevitability. The play leaves no sense that all classes involved will not remain exactly where they are. This entrenched structural resentment between an upper class and a lower class, each figured as rooted in long-standing (and non-hybrid) tradition, would become familiar.

The list of related themes threaded through private ownership of a house in David Eldridge's *In Basildon* (Royal Court, 2012) includes class, masculinity, race, work, and gender performance. Barry, a white British man in his late thirties, desires a privately owned house like his parents': the "semi-detached house in Basildon" from which the family, a generation earlier, moved from London's East End.[8] Len, the family patriarch, dies upstage in the first act, replaced in later acts by the returned living-room table—out of both of which Barry will eventually be disinherited by his Len's will. Private ownership suffuses the play: Barry calls local council flats "shit-holes," and will lament throughout his inability to acquire property: "Why shouldn't I have an [*sic*] house of my own? Why shouldn't I have a nice home to bring up a family? And be decent and normal. Everyone has got their own house except me." This failure of ownership informs Barry's racism, choleric ill humour, and physical impotence.

I've suggested that a tentative openness to change is one way that plays can embrace—or, at least, hold open a place for—the possibility of a shift in opinions, both onstage and off. *In Basildon* offers no such space for hope. Eldrige even claims Wesker's plays' influence over his own by assigning him one of the play's epigrams: "The picture I have drawn is a harsh one, yet it is not one of disgust. . . . I am at one with these people: it is only that I am annoyed, with them and myself." Yet Eldridge's play lacks Wesker's open space for future change. *In Basildon* even includes a would-be playwright character, who proposes to write "something that relates to ordinary working people. Why shouldn't they have theatre for them?" Yet the play mostly luxuriates in the smallness of its middle-England clichés, denigrating its characters through the redundancy of its description. Jackie, Barry's wife, is given the initial stage direction "*Jackie's a big woman and she's in a Tesco* uniform." Her first action is "*sharing some pickled onions from the jar*" and requesting sexual intercourse: "You know you're gonna have to give me one tonight." I do not mean to denigrate supermarket work, physical bigness, the need for sex—or, indeed, pickled onions. But the relentless piling-up of class signifiers—at one point Barry and Jackie will engage in an argument over how much salad cream Jackie consumes—absent any redeeming characteristics or countervailing personality traits dooms these characters to be the unreflective objects of something like ethnography. As Katie Beswick notes, "complexity" is one of the first causalities of theatre-makers lacking in first-hand experience of the worlds they address.[9] *In Basildon* is one of those plays where no one has any interests or hobbies beyond fulfilling what a middle-class audience would expect of their demographic—and that that is part of the point in no sense lessens the loftiness of the insult. Rather than gesture to any changed future, the last act moves 18 years into the past, showing the family's internal squabbles as in effect fated. The play narrows Barry's interests to private ownership, deprives him of it, and then retroactively shows any hope for change foreclosed by what had already happened before the play began.

Playwrights themselves often seemed to share an imaginary with poor Barry. Buying, letting, losing and scheming about private property suffuses English theatre of this decade, even in plays whose plot is not singly devoted to the topic show this influence. It is a grounding element of the reality of plays presenting abstracted, utopian, or fanciful stage worlds. No play of the 2010s seems likelier to influence other writing than Phoebe Waller-Bridge's *Fleabag* (Edinburgh Festival/Soho Theatre, 2013), whose sexually-forthright-but-emotionally-damaged monologuist has proven a template for much other work. Alongside these provocations and anxieties, *Fleabag's* central plot concerns anxiety over property rent, not of a house, but of a café. Describing a world lived partially in her head and partially in a job interview, the character equates her personal and financial near-failure to a twinned incoherence of sexual and financial purpose: "I fucked that café into liquidation."[10] Zinnie Harris' *How to Hold Your Breath* (Royal Court, 2015), an abstract refiguring of the Syrian refugee crisis around English characters, grounds its initial scenes of realism with details of property rental: the two eventual migrant sisters begin by planning a weekend trip to "look at some flats, see about our deposit." This effect becomes even more striking in Harris' subsequent *Meet Me at Dawn* (Edinburgh Festival, 2017; Arcola, 2019). Two characters meet on an island that turns out to be a kind of liminal space, one of the partners having died and the other being in mourning. Even in the void, house-buying evokes the play's longest monologue:

[D]o you remember when we looked at that house?/remember the day, we went to the pub after, we actually put the offer in from the pub and we /sat with a drink—/ we imagined every little detail of our lives/we went over and over/how we would climb the stairs at the end of the day/how we would kick off our shoes as we went into the bedroom/how we would watch the birds from the kitchen window/how we would make love in the living room/how we would sit on the stairs with hot chocolate and hot-water bottles listening to the rain.[11]

The universal becomes unimaginable without these particular experiences. Some classes have or anticipate pleasant memories of navigating owned spaces; others are brutally locked out of them. But plays of this era present few alternatives.

Mike Bartlett's *Game* (Almeida, 2015) showed a couple otherwise unable to afford a house moving in to a sort of zoo enclosure—but in a nice house—whose guests can shoot them with stun guns. An impressive experience in person, the script read subsequently makes few non-obvious points about contemporary property relations: that those with money have control over the lives of those who don't. But the immersive nature of the production, with audiences locked in to viewing areas from which actors fired on other actors in the apartment, spoke to the seeming inevitability of the property paradigm.

The Brexit decision led theatre-makers to reach towards the history and the myth—so hard to separate—of the Commons and Enclosure, whose most iconic playing-out occurred during the late eighteenth and early nineteenth centuries. The resurgence of this idea, however, played into, rather than refuted or challenged, the property paradigm of the late 2010s. The Commons story includes an inevitable fall, one that has already happened and (as a result) cannot be avoided. An old way of living in England was shattered, and the land was forever after made up of the propertied and the dispossessed. This logic forgets much of the English housing history that came between the end of the eighteenth century and the present: that, for example, as recently as the 1970s nearly a third of English people rented housing from the government.[12] As Rory Mullarkey's *St. George and the Dragon* (2017, NT) moved a nationalist pageant across three historical eras—medieval, industrial, and the present day—it moved from peasants living on what appeared to be the commons to individuals living in small private houses. DC Moore's confounding *Common* (2017), also at the NT, with its porridge of ye olde-speak and Tarantino ("What word woman? You not see I here busy wazz out my pole?"), addressed the enclosure of the commons directly.[13] Its central character, twice murdered onstage, returns to the village where she was ostracised for an apparent relationship with another woman. She has become something like capital itself, responsible for "new technology. Looms. Mills. Vast new metal-behemoths of Trade . . . Small kingdom of mymade Money." She brokers the selling of the commons, ending the influence of a wicker man-constructing local patriarchy and handing its influence over to the local squirearchy backed by London money.

Eighteen years on from *Jerusalem*, Mike Bartlett's *Albion* (Almeida, 2017) gentrified the grounds of its nationalist parable, investigating as it did the return of rural land-owning classes to their previously owned estates. The name also hints at Albion, the public school used as a national synecdoche in Alan Bennett's *Forty Years On* (1968): another claim that the country's soul can best be understood through its exclusive institutions. And indeed, *Albion* showed the whole nation as a privately owned space, one country house and its residents.

In contrast to *Jerusalem, Albion* shows female desire. Indeed, it is a play whose script calls for a woman to have onstage sex with a tree. This occurs when Anna, fiancée of the dead English soldier James, "starts . . . fucking it," as the stage directions note, in probably the most literal description of a desire to connect with family roots I have yet seen in a play. (The script leaves a lot of leeway to the staging—the script's "fucking" was, in the stage version, lessened to what Alice Saville accurately terms "humping the lawn where his ashes are scattered."[14]) That tree slash humped lawn is part of Albion, an English country estate whose private gardens were designed by a veteran of the first world war as a tribute to his fallen comrades: a past brought to life onstage by the music of Victorian composer Edward Elgar (1857–1934), rather than Rooster's drum 'n' bass. These gardens are restored to life, briefly, by Audrey Walters, a home furnishings magnate who has sold her London house for a chance to restore this country estate. Her son has died in the Iraq war; his fiancée becomes mysteriously pregnant. They come together in some sort of mystical communion with the garden, whence the sex with the tree.

A decade of austerity stands between *Jerusalem* and *Albion*. (It almost sounds like a song lyric, the mythological diversities of the former becoming the austere whiteness of the latter.) The legal owner of the private land on which she stands, Audrey walks through the script uttering a series of regressive observations:

Audrey: My uncle had staff when he was here. I remember being fascinated when we came to visit. Where did they go?! But no, I mean all that . . . long gone . . . although I do find myself thinking what exactly is wrong with it? As long as they're paid well, are happy in their jobs, they would have more security than a courier or one of those Uber drivers. A part of me doesn't understand why it's politically incorrect.

Audrey is upbraided for these opinions—she will be reminded that the twenties were politically terrible, and that people suffered in the service. But played by Victoria Hamilton, well known on television and in the theatre, Audrey is (like the Rylance-portrayed Rooster) the centre of the play's focus. The play will indeed include an outwardly contented service worker, the Polish cleaning-service entrepreneur Krystyna, happy to serve drinks in a 1920s gown. Audrey's point about Uber drivers got one of those "hmms" you occasionally get at well-made points in well-made plays, the Islington audience earnestly considering a return to feudalism. Audrey's interests may well be outmoded or even delusional—as other characters remark—but they are what *Albion* spends most of its running time discussing. In 11 years, the figure bearing the weight of English nostalgia shifted from a male sexual abuser to a female home furnisher entrepreneur surrounded by deferential foreigners and a grandchild inferentially born of tree—or, maybe more charitably, of deep-rooted connection with the English earth of a country estate.

 Albion ends in an ambiguous despair: in *Ragnarök* written by an estate agent. Unable to financially support Albion, Audrey signs a contract to sell it off to the housing developers who lurk like nemesis about the contemporary agrarian drama. Her daughter calls this "democracy," but Audrey depicts this as the end of the earth. This time, there's no mention of council involvement. The flats, as Audrey envisions them, will be "buy-to-lets and holidays mostly," not houses for "couples and family" possessing "a home of their own for the first time." But this property-based pessimism extends further, into something like her vision of the country itself:

> Even with death most things carry on. Plants seed, children are born. Inheritance. One generation after another. But there is a time when that stops. When for one reason or another a species dies. A culture expires. That particular line of history comes to an end. I know you, and your friends, and Katherine, you all laughed at me for wanting to do this, but don't you think there was something, in all this, that was worth preserving? That some part of it, just some little part of it, might be *good*?

In Audrey's vision, "this"—an inchoate but capacious notion of Englishness—"expires" when the estate is sold. It's all or nothing: we can't keep, say, reggae, shoemaking, and *Cold Comfort Farm*, and leave behind caning, statues of sla-veowners, and cap-doffing deference. The speech moves up and down a scale of abstractions: now a "species," now a "culture," now a "line of history," now "something . . . some little part of it." The rejection of Albion *in toto* is seemingly the rejection of all of these things. A holiday home would have no access to this Chthonic national imaginary.

The country, thusly figured, has let Audrey down. She rattles off a list of issues:

> [T]he house . . . requires hundreds of thousands of pounds of work, just to stay up. And the garden even more. Groundwater. Disease in half the trees. Miner bees everywhere. Ants. There's some things you can't restore. The earth itself.

This flirting with national themes, the coy echo of the miner's strikes, this figur-ing of population as rotting ecology, framed the country entirely around her class interests. What she laments on some level is the land's inability to snap to her particular world view: the way that it instead presents complexity, a lack of bid-dability, and resistance. At the last moment, Audrey has a change of heart, decid-ing this vision of England may be saved: "This is everything. Myself. My family. James. My past. My future. I don't want anything else but this piece of land." She seems at this moment a tragic figure: as the stage directions confirm, "She doesn't know what she's doing." Like Bill from the North-East in *My Country: A Work in Progress*, Audrey winds up in the cold dirt, working at something she doesn't understand but blithely continuing on.

Maybe she just needs another hobby.

Anxieties can have a luxurious component. They envelop us in regression; they let us fixate and ruminate. Equally, they can keep us from moving forward. All of *Albion's* psychological action, its returned war dead and affective tree-fucking, depends on the persistence of the intact estate. The play gives its last lines to Matthew, the former groundskeeper (and working-class stand-in) suffering from dementia: "We have to keep it!/I've been watching. . . . [T]here's something in the air./Don't you think?" Leaving aside the strange politics of figuring demented characters as plot points—something weirdly common in the theatre of the later decade—the assignment of any sort of countervailing hope only to a character lacking full mental capacities typifies a theatre disengaging or demolishing criti-cal or alternative perspectives.[15] This England has no soul without the unending psychic playing-out of Enclosure, but no future within its privatised structures. Its future may be private ownership without this soul; but any alternatives offered by its past, including the possibility of any sort of collective solution, have simply been erased. This affective crux committed English playwrights to a seemingly inescapable pessimism: a set of false binaries, a zero-sum game.

This might not have seemed like a hopeful book. But it was written out of a sense, however faint, of hope: that theatre could do better than track a prevail-ing, regressive mindset. Parallel accounts of theatre in this period are possible, particularly when unscripted drama is considered. But for those unable to access performance pieces directly, it can be frankly difficult to write histories of the English stage outside of what appears in the major venues in which scripted drama predominates. Two of the best plays that I saw during these years, refigurings of England's collective and industrial past in Manchester, both appeared at that city's Royal Exchange Theatre. The account of a protest by 1990s miners' wives in *Queens of the Coal Age* (2018), and of the Luddite rebellion in *There Is A Light That Never Goes Out* (2019), are both hard to write about, because their scripts never made it to print. More particularly, neither of these plays made claims to be State of England dramas, in the way that *Jerusalem* or *Albion* attempted.

There would be other ways to tell this story—other moments where property relations did not kick up English theatre's most entrenched positions regarding how people interact with one another. There's a part in Ambreen Razia's *The Diary of a Hounslow Girl* (Ovalhouse, 2016), a solo play for a female performer about a Pakistani-British Muslim teenager, that both recapitulates this property paradigm but also, maybe, holds a space open for something beyond it. Early in the play, Shaheeda, the girl of the title, ventriloquises her mother critiquing a friend's allocation of a council flat, allotted following the friend's pregnancy with an "English boy":

> Your Auntie Nusrut told me that her niece went on *Facebook*—she met a boy and ran off with him! Now they're living in a council house in Hackbridge. One of those small one-bedroom flats with no double glazing and electric cookers.[16]

Anyone who has spent any time in cheap English accommodations knows, viscerally, the smell of dust being incinerated on an electric cooker element; seemingly anyone who has spent any time in English conversation has been spoken to earnestly about double glazing. Shaheeda addresses this world, in which every housing microtransaction is scrutinised and visible. I think the play also gestures towards something else, if inchoately. Bruised by heartache, cultural in-betweenness, and her own family members' fists following her own eventual pregnancy, Shaheeda nevertheless concludes the play hopefully:

> The feelings I have now won't disappear overnight, but somehow, someway. . . . [E]verything will be alright. (She smiles to herself.) I ain't dumb. I'm intelligent enough to know, that I don't know anything. And do you know what? I think that might get me through.

Razia's play is restless with old narratives, but she does not seem hopeless that her character will repeat them. There's nothing in Shaheeda's story to which a narrative of the Commons could be applied—indeed, as her mother keeps telling her, "You're a Muslim girl. Remember, Shaheeda—you may be British, but you are not English." This is a complicated statement: a very specific community's claim to representative status within an international tradition, albeit an imperial one; a refusal of one kind of English localness. And Shaheeda is not her mother—nor is she English, at least as Englishness is defined as having imagined human roots back to the Commons. She repeats her mother's condemnation of social housing—it's what people in London talk about—but this talk is not the sum total of how she sees herself. Something hybrid, and something hopeful, may endure. And this hope reopens the possibility of an alternate teleology—or other alternate teleologies—of what the stage could do. "I'm guaranteed first-hand wisdom," she claims, "and I can actually be taught something without someone having to teach me." The yearning for experience, presented without a particular consensus of what form that experience will take, takes us back to Wesker, and to the future-anterior urgency of what his play calls for: that there are things that ought to be done. But it happened in a one-person show that, although touring nationally and widely throughout London, never brought its main character into conversation with anyone else. It might be possible to bring *Hounslow Girl's* perspective into a framing where it might serve as a national parable: a bigger cast, a larger stage, and a more expansive framing. After all, *Roots* did something similar. For this to happen, I suggest in conclusion, private property ownership needs to stop being the emotional arena—and the literal and figurative ground—for so much of national cultural life.

Notes

1 *Jerusalem* was, for example, declared in 2019 the best play of the century so far by the *Guardian*. Alexis Soloski Michael Billington, Catherine Love, Mark Fisher, and Chris Wiegand, "The 50 Best Theatre Shows of the 21st Century," *The Guardian* (London), September 17, 2019, www.theguardian.com/stage/2019/sep/17/the-50-best-theatre-shows-of-the-21st-century.
2 Jez Butterworth, *Jerusalem* (Nick Hern Books, 2009), https://doi.org/10.5040/9781784600044.00000003. Written during COVID lockdown, this chapter needed to use online texts.
3 Jill Dolan, *The Feminist Spectator as Critic*, 2nd ed. (Ann Arbor: University of Michigan Press, 2012), xxv. Dolan addresses the production's New York transfer.
4 April De Angelis, "Troubling Gender on Stage and with the Critics," *Theatre Journal* 62, no. 4 (2010): 559.
5 Katie Beswick, *Social Housing in Performance* (London: Methuen, 2019), 109.
6 "Speech on Public Services," *The Guardian*, 2001, www.theguardian.com/politics/2001/may/21/labour.tonyblair.
7 Imogen Tyler, *Revolting Subjects: Social Abjection and Resistance in Neoliberal Britain* (London: Zed Books Ltd., 2013), 12 and passim.
8 David Eldridge, *In Basildon* (Bloomsbury Publishing, 2012), https://doi.org/10.5040/9781408174975.00000002.
9 Katie Beswick, *Social Housing in Performance* (London: Methuen, 2019), 11. Beswick describes characters on social housing estates, but the effect is equivalent.
10 Phoebe Waller-Bridge, *Fleabag* (Nick Hern Books, 2013), https://doi.org/10.5040/9781784601942.00000002.
11 Zinnie Harris, *Meet Me at Dawn* (Faber and Faber, 2017), https://doi.org/10.5040/9780571347339.00000003.
12 James Meek, *Private Island* (London: Verso, 2014).

13 D.C. Moore, *Common* (Bloomsbury Publishing, 2017), https://doi.org/10.5040/97813
50042490.00000003.

14 Alice Saville, "Albion Review," *Time Out London* (London), February 6, 2020, www.
timeout.com/london/theatre/albion-review.

15 Later-life diseases and the possibilities they offer introducing the component of an
unstable or unreliable narrator appeared in, in a quick recollection, Sam Mendes' staging of *King Lear* (NT, 2014), Florian Zeller's, *The Father* (Kiln, 2015), and Arthur
Kopit's *Wings* at the Young Vic (2017).

16 Ambreen Razia, *The Diary of a Hounslow Girl* (Aurora Metro Books, 2016), https://
doi.org/10.5040/9781911501770.00000002.

Works cited

Angelis, April. "Troubling Gender on Stage and with the Critics." *Theatre Journal* 62, no.
4 (2010): 557–9.

Beswick, Katie. *Social Housing in Performance*. London: Methuen, 2019.

Blair, Tony. "Speech on Public Services." *The Guardian*, 2001. www.theguardian.com/
politics/2001/may/21/labour.tonyblair.

Butterworth, Jez. *Jerusalem*. Nick Hern Books, 2009. https://doi.org/10.5040/978178460
0044.00000003.

Dolan, Jill. *The Feminist Spectator as Critic*. 2nd ed. Ann Arbor: University of Michigan
Press, 2012.

Eldridge, David. *In Basildon*. Bloomsbury Publishing, 2012. https://doi.org/10.5040/9781
408174975.00000002.

Harris, Zinnie. *Meet Me at Dawn*. Faber and Faber, 2017. https://doi.org/10.5040/978057
1347339.00000003.

Meek, James. *Private Island, Electronic Book*. London: Verso, 2014.

Michael Billington, Alexis Soloski, Catherine Love, Mark Fisher, and Chris Wiegand. "The
50 Best Theatre Shows of the 21st Century." *The Guardian* (London), September 17,
2019. www.theguardian.com/stage/2019/sep/17/the-50-best-theatre-shows-of-the-21st-
century.

Moore, D.C. *Common*. Bloomsbury Publishing, 2017. https://doi.org/10.5040/978135004
2490.00000003.

Razia, Ambreen. *The Diary of a Hounslow Girl*. Aurora Metro Books, 2016. https://doi.org
/10.5040/9781911501770.00000002.

Saville, Alice. "Albion Review." *Time Out London* (London), February 6, 2020. www.
timeout.com/london/theatre/albion-review.

Tyler, Imogen. *Revolting Subjects: Social Abjection and Resistance in Neoliberal Britain*.
London: Zed Books Ltd., 2013.

Waller-Bridge, Phoebe. *Fleabag*. Nick Hern Books, 2013. https://doi.org/10.5040/978178
4601942.00000002.

Index

Lightning Source UK Ltd.
Milton Keynes UK
UKHW020758010822
406672UK00006B/661